SCHUYLER SPIRITUAL SERIES
Vol. 3

INTIMACY WITH GOD

Notes on the Vocation to Celibacy

Clifford Stevens

BMH Publications
Benedictine Mission House
Box 528
Schuyler, Nebraska 68661-0528

Nihil Obstat:
Val J. Peter, JCD, STD
June 2, 1992

Imprimatur:
Daniel E. Sheehan
Archbishop of Omaha

"For friends to converse together is the proper condition of friendship. Men's conversation with God is through contemplation. The Holy Spirit makes us God's lovers."

"Eternal life consists in enjoying God."

"We shall be like a lover who has long searched, and at last the Beloved is found."

"Virtue is called the limit of potentiality. . . because it causes an inclination to the highest act a faculty can perform."

"By loving God, we glow to gaze on His beauty."

. . . Saint Thomas Aquinas

For David Ricken

Stay in the splendor,
Your fierce lamps blazing,
Ascending the footsteps of the morning
To where your dreams have entered.

+ CONTENTS +

PREFATORY NOTES

The author of "Intimacy with God" and "The Noblest Love" sees a common purpose and a close comparison between the two paths of celibacy and marriage; therefore, some of the material, which he feels belong and are central to each, occurs in both volumes.

Since no stylistically strong neuter substitute for the masculine generalization has been established, for the integrity of style we have elected to keep the masculine pronomial whenever a genderless antecedent is established. Hence, sentences read: "The celibate. . . he. . . ."

The terms "sex" and "sexual intimacy" appear frequently throughout these pages. In general, the reference is to *genital* sexuality in marriage. It is recognized that we are all sexual beings and that intimacy is normal, necessary and beautiful in any relationship. . . Just as intimacy with God is not the privilege of the celibate alone, intimacy with other human beings is not the privilege solely of married couples. The author holds, however, that the celibate commitment allows an intimacy with God of a *particular* nature, which is balanced by and has its counterpart only in the particular intimacy between committed, consecrated lovers. Just as a celibate can learn through his particular intimacy how to grow in his love for human beings, so can the married person grow in love of God by focusing their love on another human being. All poetry not otherwise noted is the author's own.

[-- the editor --]

INTRODUCTION

I have always found books on celibacy just a bit too serious, and perhaps a bit too scholarly, far removed from the world I live in and far removed as well from my own motivation in taking on a life of celibacy. I have often wondered why it must be so. Perhaps it is the 19th century genre of spiritual writing that is to blame, perhaps it is the philosophical presuppositions behind these learned treatises, but I have always found them just a little bit unreal, filled at the same time with dire warnings and exhortations that I have found slightly intimidating.

I am sure that mine is not a lone experience. I have just never taken myself as seriously as these writings seem to demand, and celibacy, when I looked it straight in the eye, I found friendly and sensible and a good companion for the kind of priestly life that I wanted to live. That does not mean that I have not had questions about it, or tried to probe its rationale, but I have never found celibacy itself the heavy, ponderous thing certain books seem to assume. If one can fall lightheartedly in love and still face with mature responsibility the labor of raising a family, one can face the celibate life with the same lightheartedness and sense of joy. The asceticism required for celibacy is no more burdensome than that required for marriage, even though it has its own particular style and its own kind of vigilance. What I have disagreed with at times is the implication that celibacy is somehow superior to marriage. I could plainly see myself in both situations, and I could never understand why one made me superior to the other.

What I have especially found, as my own ponderings on the subject gave me firm convictions, is that behind much discussion of celibacy was a highly defective view of sexuality, if there was any at all, and that I simply could not identify with the negative spirituality behind such exhortation to celibacy. It was based on a view of sexuality that I have never been comfortable with and I have found it totally inadequate in articulating a spirituality of celibacy.

What inspired this book were conversations with young priests and seminarians who were curious about this ancient discipline and wondered about the *rationale* behind it. Their constant complaint was that they had encountered no real "theology of celibacy", and that most treatments of the subject were subtle put-downs of sexuality and marriage: trying "to make something negative, positive." "There is no spirituality of celibacy," one of them told me, "there is only a spirituality of non-sexuality, of 'sexlessness', with a few vague references to 'celibacy for the Kingdom of God'."

There is nothing mystical or mysterious or enigmatic about celibacy in itself: it is the simple renunciation of one of the most glorious experiences in human life, the genital expression of sexual intimacy between a man and woman in marriage. It has been the custom in the past to downgrade and belittle this experience, as if there were something essentially unwholesome and degrading about it, thereby making the choice of celibacy more attractive and cogent. The anthropology behind this kind of celibate "spirituality" is highly defective and the "spirituality" itself totally invalid. What is being rejected today is, perhaps, not the celibate commitment itself, but this defective anthropology and this highly intimidating spirituality.

The older celibate spirituality tended to be somewhat negative about marriage and sexual intimacy and no one has to accept that kind of reasoning today. It was understandable in an age when marriage was considered merely a "way of salvation" and celibacy a "way of holiness." Whether intended or not, this was a subtle put-down of married love and conjugal intimacy, as if these were held in disfavor in God's eyes. Today it is realized that holiness is the goal of every form of Christian life and that sexual intimacy in marriage is as valid a pathway to holiness as consecrated celibacy. They are two sides of the same coin.

Reflection on celibacy must necessarily include reflection on sexuality, on one's own sexuality and on the place of sexuality in the life of man and woman. This study opens with a positive and affirmative view of human sexuality and of the sexual intimacy to which it leads. Celibacy must be based on a profound appreciation for the gift of sexual intimacy, as a personal gift and endowment from God, and as an integral part of one's masculine or feminine inheritance. Only then does the specific character of consecrated celibacy begin to be seen.

In the Aquinas tradition, which distills the exhilarating vision of the Christian Revelation and the instinct for *arete*, "excellence", of the ancient Greeks, a young man is given a passion for what is noble and good, but is taught not to hide from himself, nor is there hidden from him the full implications of his naked manhood, his naked intelligence, and his naked masculinity.

Nobility of soul does not fail to plumb and to appreciate the riches of either the masculine or the feminine possibility which is the natural inheritance of an awakened and full adulthood. It is one of the premises of this book that one can possess one's sexuality in complete innocence, with a wholesome sense of dignity, freedom, wonder, and joy in its possession, and look forward to and experience its joyous expression in marriage, with the same complete innocence.

This possibility, with all its splendor and enrichment, does not exhaust the human possibility, but it does enshrine some of its noblest instincts, a panoply of its keenest passions--of the feelings and of the mind--and an intimacy that mirrors the very loving vitality of God's own self.

Mankind's noblest earthly love must be seen and recognized in all its beauty and all its human possibilities if the nobler love is to have any meaning at all. As a celibate, I set aside sexual intimacy with a woman, with all its rooms of joy and beauty, only for a greater intimacy and its even more wondrous rooms of beauty, and its universe of joy. But in doing so, I cannot and I will not deny the power, the significance or the magnitude of the masculine expectancy that I set aside and turn away from. That intimacy, by whatever name it is called, is riveted into my very flesh, the lineaments of its passionate preoccupation are traced and interlaced in the very warp and woof of my biology.

The pattern of the sexual encounter is the most obvious fact of my physical being. I am shaped and fashioned by every ripple and nuance of my living flesh for physical intimacy with a woman. To hide this from myself in the name of celibacy would rob the choice of celibacy of half its meaning.

I am created for beatitude; that is what I affirm in my choice of celibacy. But it is more than affirmation; it is a step in that direction, not by the static and anguished deprivation of my physical and masculine inheritance, but by the very savoring of that beatitude as I reach out to intimacy with God.

The gift of manhood with all its passionate possibilities is one of the richest gifts of God. I set its sexual expression aside freely, not without appreciation for its beauty, and not with regret, but because I have stumbled onto a greater beauty, a more powerful intimacy, and a more earth-shaking encounter. In the shadow of that intimacy and shaken with this expectancy, every other possibility fades into insignificance.

Sex, sexual love and sex experience lose nothing of their power and beauty; but in my encounter with a deathless, timeless and ageless God, I find a bride and consort for my spirit and a flaming passion for my mind fully as equal in its intensity as the full sexual encounter of man and woman.

I do not hide from myself the shattering loveliness and raw beauty of the sexual intimacy that could be mine, but celibacy reaches out to something greater, fully as rich, fully as valid, and as fully a complement to my manhood as the rich experience of love in marriage.

The song of celibacy is fully as rich as the love-song of man and woman, and the intimacy that inspires it has been the theme of mystics from time immemorial. The celibate, no less than the married man, is primarily a lover.

It is this vision of celibacy that needs to be recaptured, but a vision of celibacy based upon a profound appreciation for the gift of sexuality and the gift of human love.

Sleeping Alone

The most obvious fact about a celibate is that he "sleeps alone". It is the most obvious and, to some, the most puzzling thing about him because it is not clear why he would want to do such a thing. After all, sleeping with someone is a perfectly respectable thing to do and is the normal occupation of millions of men and women. Sleeping alone does not seem to make any sense, or at least it seems to unduly complicate the business of living. The motivation escapes a lot of people and seems to them an unhealthy rejection of life and of one of the loveliest experiences of the human condition.

"Sleeping alone", in this sense, has nothing to do with a hatred of life or with an insensitivity to the sexual or with some kind of antipathy towards the opposite sex. There have been celibates who were motivated by this kind of thinking and early Christianity is full of them. But no one takes that sort of thing seriously anymore.

The celibate, constitutionally, is as "sexy" as any other human being, and his biological orientation towards sex is the most obvious fact of his nature. He can no more ignore it than he can ignore the need to eat or sleep or the need to converse or the joy that he has in friends and loved ones. Affectively and emotionally, he is like any other person, with a body like other people, and, if he has not been jaded by a false asceticism, just as appreciative of beauty and the joys of sex as any other member of the species.

Celibacy is not a *denial* of anything. It is rather an *affirmation* of something beyond the sexual, the earthly and the here and now. It is not linked in its roots to the virtue of chastity at all but to *magnificence,*[1] a certain exhuberance in living, a bursting of the bonds of the ordinary to reach out to the extraordinary. It is based on a hunger for the eternal and for an intimacy as real and as stunning as the intimacy of man and woman in marriage.

In choosing to "sleep alone", I was not conscious of saying to myself: "I will never have a woman in my life; I will never know the joy of going to bed with a woman or of sleeping in the arms of my bride on our wedding night." This never crossed my mind, even though it was implicit in the decision I made. I was conscious of being fascinated with God, of entering into a profound and intense solitude with Him, and of feeling joy to the very roots of my being at the thought of this lifelong association. I never consciously excluded a woman from my life and from my bed; I just did not include her.

For some people, of course, these things simply should not be talked about, and so I do not address myself to them. After all, I have brothers and sisters who are married, who have children, who sleep with their husbands and wives, and, under different circumstances I would have done the same, had a wife and children of my own and found myself sleeping with a woman as my habitual occupation. The fact that I have not is simply the fact that I have not. My celibacy has nothing to do with any negative judgment about these things or any embarrassment in the face of them.

I have never understood why these things should be embarrassing or unseemly to talk about. As a young boy, eleven or twelve years of age, roving with boy companions along the shores of the Connecticut River in Vermont, we used to swim in the *altogether*, and, tanned from head to toe, roam over our Connecticut River island as naked as South Sea Island natives, with no sense of shame and a rollicking sense of fun that delights me to this day. Even then, I understood, or at least half-sensed, that my boyish animality was a splendid gift of God and I sensed something of the delight I could have with my body with the coming of full manhood, and I saw this as somehow connected with my sexuality.

I never saw any indecency in this, but only a sense of wonder at the goodness of God Who had planned that even my body should experience something of His goodness. That is how I looked upon it then and that is how I look upon it now, even though my knowledge of that experience and my understanding of the full meaning of that delight has deepened considerably. Nevertheless, it still leaves me in awe. My choice of celibacy when I reached full manhood had nothing to do with any less appreciation for this gift or any rejection of my sexuality.

In growing up, I had simply never come across the woman I would share my life and bed with, for the simple reason that my life took an entirely different direction. Sleeping alone has nothing to do with any lack of appreciation for the joy of sleeping with a woman. In sleeping alone, I wrapped myself in a personal solitude that only God inhabits and cultivated habits of intimacy that strike to the very roots of my existence. If the joy and ecstasy of sex, in the words of Dietrich von Hildebrand, "go to the very depths of bodily existence"[2] the joy of intimacy with God goes to the very depths of your total existence and calls into play all the powers of your being. The celibate does not inhabit his solitude alone, any more than the married person does. His solitude is inhabited by God in a profoundly personal way that simply cannot be expressed.

What impressed me about my sexuality, when I began to reflect upon it in later years, was that God had intended and planned for me to be intimate with a woman. That possibility and the pattern of that intimacy were molded into my very body and I was profoundly impressed with the fact that He had planned and designed this intimacy to be part of my personal pursuit of happiness. The fact that I did not have a woman in my life was *my* choosing, not His, even though His Providence obviously had something to do with it, as celibacy is as much a *gift* as it is a personal choice. But the gift of sexual joy was never denied me. I simply took another direction by my own choice and initiative. From my biological and physical constitution, God intended for me to be intimate with a woman in the ecstasy of sex and He made this intimacy and this ecstasy part of my masculine inheritance. Such delicate concern for my own personal happiness gave me a new insight into God's goodness and a new appreciation for the gift of marriage that could have been mine.

It is unfortunate that in the history of Christian spirituality the vocation to celibacy has often been explained in terms that denigrate the value and beauty of sexual love in marriage. The impression is given that the choice of celibacy is somehow a flight from something radically unspiritual, and that the celibate looks upon conjugal intimacy as something beneath his dignity, something that would mar his perfect purity. The choice of celibacy, if it is genuine, has nothing of this motivation about it, but is based solidly and squarely on something more positive and something more exhilarating.

To put it bluntly, the celibate is broken with the beauty of God. Celibacy is a step in the direction of intimacy with God, not because marriage and sexual love are necessarily an obstacle to this, but simply because celibacy provides that total personal solitude from which he can cultivate an exclusive intimacy with God. It is his vocation to bear witness to the overpowering reality of God.

His celibacy does not bear witness to the absence of sex in his life, even though it includes this. It is primarily a symbol of his total consecration to God and eternal things and flows therefore from an exuberance of love, which sets the tone for the whole vocation of celibacy.

It is a basic premise of this book that one can possess one's sexuality in complete innocence, with a wholesome sense of dignity, freedom, wonder and joy in its possession, and can be profoundly appreciative, even as a celibate, of its joyous expression in the intimacy of marriage, with the same complete innocence. I am convinced that most celibates choose a life of celibacy first and then reflect upon it, their reflections having little to do with their original motivation. What is important, it seems to me, is the *rationale* that is given for the choice of celibacy, once reflection upon it has begun, and that this *rationale* be based upon a sound anthropology and upon a view of sexuality that is positive and genuinely human. From this positive base, the beginnings of a theology and spirituality of celibacy can be glimpsed and the true dimensions of the vocation to celibacy begin to be seen.

The rest is part of that primitive face we show only to God.

I
Sexuality and the Sacredness of the Human

Any study of celibacy must examine the role of sex in human affairs, since celibacy, in its content, turns aside from the sexual encounter of man and woman in marriage, and from the sexual intimacy which is the heart of married love. What is demanded at the very beginning of a study of celibacy is a theology of human sexuality which is in keeping with the ordinary experience of men and women, and which makes sense to a creature endowed with sexuality.[1] Any approach to celibacy which rejects the values inherent in sexual love or belittles its significance in human life becomes less credible the more it is examined. And any theology of celibacy which hints or teaches that sexual love, in all its passionate beauty, is unworthy of the spiritual man, contains the seeds of its own destruction, and will never be convincing to intelligently informed men and women. What the celibate must see is that the choice of celibacy is not a denial or rejection of his own sexuality, and that the consciousness of this sexuality and of its breathtaking possibilities, is not contrary to a strong and genuine celibacy.

Any belittling of sexual love undermines the very splendor of the celibate dedication. If sex is cheap and worthless, the instinctive carrying out of "the desires of the flesh," then any withdrawal from sexual activity is not only desirable, it is even demanded by the spiritual man. Sexual love then becomes the refuge of the weak, a "remedy for concupiscence," the indulgence of a basically selfish instinct, redeemed only by procreation.

That this has often been the evaluation placed upon human sexuality by theologians, there can be no doubt. That this is an unworthy belittling of the most moving of all human relationships is the first conviction of the genuine theologian. A true theology of celibacy does not look upon the sexual intimacy of man and woman in marriage as unworthy of the spiritual man. Rather, it tries to integrate sex into a vision of Christian holiness. Anything else is a vicious attack upon a basic human experience, and a celibacy which does not recognize sex in all its passionate beauty and breathtaking joy as eminently good, is not worthy of the God "Who was made flesh and dwelt amongst us." Sex is not something that is beneath the dignity of the celibate, something that would somehow mar his perfect purity. It is the basic human experience, created, designed and shaped in all its physical and psychological elements by God Himself.

Sex is indeed the finest and most genuine expression of masculinity and femininity and enriches human life immeasurably. In its true psychological, physical, spiritual and physical totality it has a power, a beauty, a splendor all its own and is an activity eminently worthy and desirable. It is the deepest and most intimate union of two human beings possible on earth[2] and in its depth and intensity mirrors God's own love for human beings.

"Sex" is an encounter, strange and magnificent, between two human beings[3] conscious of the riches of their own sexuality. It is a communion of two human beings, a man and a woman, bringing to their intimate union the full wealth of their physical, psychological, emotional and spiritual beings. It is the sealing of two plighted lovers in an intimate and enriching rite eminently worthy and desirable.

In all its raw and naked beauty, sex is an enriching, vivifying and strengthening experience: enriching the human person, vivifying the love of husband and wife, and strengthening and enlivening the bond of married friendship.[4]

It is by acts of sexual love, in all their intimate reality, that a man fulfills uniquely his three-fold role of father, husband and lover; and a woman hers of mother, wife and lover. Sex is at once a creative act of great depth and beauty, an intimate sharing of a wondrous mystery, and the sealing of a tender and passionate friendship.[5]

This evaluation of sexual love is drawn straight from Divine Revelation and from human experience, and the richest source of this theology is the divinely-inspired *Song of Songs*, which is a frank description of the sexual encounter of man and woman and an intimate revelation of the erotic dimension in human life.[6] Sex, even for the celibate, must be seen as the design of God, the work of God and the glory of God, and any sound choice of celibacy must be based upon an awareness of its significance in the life of man or woman.

Such an evaluation of its role in the life of man and woman is part and parcel of genuine holiness and is necessary if a proper appreciation of celibacy is to be grasped. For the celibate is destined in his physical and spiritual being for this intimacy and this communion and the fact that he does not choose to integrate this total experience into his life does not change the orientation of his nature.

However, the breathtaking beauty of sexual love does not make its choice a necessity, for there is a whole complex of social, psychological and affective factors that enter into the choice of conjugal love. The celibate does not change his sexual nature, he simply chooses not to include sexual activity in his life . . . for reasons that have value for him and for him alone. But the reality of sex is there, and his celibacy should not exclude a profound appreciation of its riches.

For the sake of Christian spirituality, it must be stated clearly and unequivocally: there is nothing in human sexuality or in its full genuine expression in marriage that is contrary to genuine holiness. The value of celibacy is not based upon its quality of sexlessness. Nor is it necessary to approach human love cautiously and nervously, as if there were anything about it which is an obstacle to the highest sanctity. It is, in all its wonder and beauty, the creation and the gift of God and possesses a sacredness and a sanctifying power worthy of the purest of saints.

This vision of human sexuality and of married love did not receive explicit expression in Catholic theology until recently, in spite of the pioneer efforts of St. Thomas Aquinas in his study of human nature. The words of the Second Vatican Council that "*the acts by which the couple are united intimately and chastely are noble and worthy*"[7] are something entirely new in official Catholic thought, even though this had been the common conviction of many Catholics for centuries. In this document, Catholic theology finally broke away from the pessimism and stoicism of St. Augustine. The Council goes on to say that "those actions signify and nourish that mutual self-surrender by which men and women enrich each other with a joyful and grateful goodwill."[8]

It is amazing that Catholic theology took so many centuries to come to a proper appreciation of human sexuality. The fact that the majority of men and women are married seemed to have had little effect upon the theology of previous centuries. Much of the pessimism that crept into theology regarding sex and marriage had its roots in the *Augustinian* tradition which came close to Gnosticism in its evaluation of human nature.[9] At the bottom of the new theology of sex and married love is a view of holiness which has a deep reverence for the human, a theology reflected so well in the *Pastoral Constitution on the Church in the Modern World* ("Gaudium et Spes") of the Second Vatican Council. It has its roots also in patristic and theological thought as, for example, the theological genius of St. Thomas Aquinas, who in his thought had a profound respect for the human, and who, in his own lifetime[10] parted company with that theological tradition which constantly belittled the human and saw no value in human achievement or in human knowledge. Consider these statements from his anthropological insights:

"By the friendship of charity, by which we love God, we should cherish the body."
(S. T., II-II, Q. 25.)

"Every movement of sense desire conformed to true knowledge is good in itself."
(S. T., II-II, Q. 20.)

"Moral virtue perfects sense desire by directing it towards the good of reason."
(S. T., I-II, Q. 59.)

"Moral virtue is nothing other than the participation of sense desire in right reason."
(Q.D. de Virt. Comm., 12.)

"Pleasure perfects operation as beauty perfects youth. The more perfect the operation, the more perfect the pleasure."
(S. T., I-II, Q. 32.)

"He who avoids pleasure because it is pleasurable is boorish and ungracious."
(S. T., II-II, Q. 42.)

"Delight is not best just because it is delight, but because it is repose with the best."
(S. T., I-II, Q. 34.)

"Delight of mind does not clog the use of reason; on the contrary, we are more intent on what we more enjoy."
(S. T., I-II, Q. 33.)

"In us there is not only the pleasure we share with other living things, but also the pleasure we share with the angels."
(S. T., I-II, Q. 31.)

"There is no free play of the mind except where the senses are fit and vigorous."
(II ad Corinth., 12, lect. 1.)

In his theological writings, St. Thomas (let us stay with him) indicated that nothing truly human is outside the scope of holiness, and he emphasized the fact that what is truly human has a value and a sacredness all its own, quite apart from its place in the spiritual life. This principle of St. Thomas and of a genuinely Catholic philosophy was never really taken seriously by many older spiritual writers. If they touched on it, it was only in passing, and the full implications of the principle have come to light only in our time.

Holiness and humanness are closely bound up with each other, and genuine holiness makes for a more complete human being. It is important in this age of blossoming human genius to insist that holiness is not lived in a vacuum, but is essentially bound up within a definite human context, and that those human values which are an integral part of normal human living lose nothing of their beauty and value when touched by the Christian vision.

Spirituality in the past tended towards an asceticism of pessimism with regard to human nature, and in consequence usually bred holiness in a vacuum, and the perfection that was placed before the mind was that of a flawless morality or ascetic mastery. Saints, it seemed, were giants precisely because they withdrew from the earthly and the human.

We cannot deny that this conclusion was part of these spiritualities and that these spiritualities did produce men and women of genuine and heroic sanctity. However, we must also admit that this vision of holiness is severely limited and, in some respects, neither genuinely Christian nor theologically sound. A sound view of holiness recognizes the essential sacredness of the human, even apart from the supernatural life that makes it an instrument of grace; and disavows the claim that whatever is not genuinely human cannot be brought into the orbit of our relationship with God.

In the stark and serious (and highly adventurous) business of building the City of Man, we must be conscious that with the same tools we can build the City of God. The human adventure and the drama of living, broadening as they are in this age of technology, are part of a greater and more lasting adventure, bringing human beings eventually to the very vision and possession of God. With a firm grasp upon human dignity, we begin to catch a breathtaking glimpse of human destiny: to belittle anything genuinely human is to cheapen the dignity of the human person and, in consequence, the vision of human destiny.

St. Thomas expressed this conviction in a number of ways, most of them deeply philosophical. In one passage, however, he touches upon the heart of the matter when he says: "contemplation is good for the soul, but so is a good warm bath." We must insist that there is holiness in everything, that there is nothing in the whole of human life which a saint cannot touch and make part of his life. There is a holy way to pray and to sing and to dance; there is a holy way to work and drink beer and make love; there is a holy way to play tennis and marry and wash dishes. The scope of holiness is as broad as human experience itself and any action which is not in itself sinful can be made part of our search for God.

One of the consequences of the older view of holiness was the gradual separation of holiness and life: holiness was for monks and nuns in monasteries and for other-worldly mystics, holiness was a flight from the human. There was no attempt to confront genuine human problems. Gradually the art of holiness became a mere ascetic or devotional exercise, completely unrelated to any real human situation: mapped out, catalogued, neatly labeled. One had to choose between being holy and being human.

The early studies in psychology and the gradual growth of science and technology began to reveal the flaw in this vision of our relationship with God. And soon genuinely religious people were faced with a strange dilemma: human affairs increasingly demanded talent, intelligence, nerve, decision and sinewed skill, calling upon all that was best and noblest in human beings; religion too often demanded only an emasculated response, passive and impersonal. Right before their eyes there seemed to be fulfilled the words of Jesus Himself: *The children of this world are wiser in their generation than the children of light.*

Genuine holiness has no small estimate of human achievement, and is not a mere critic and observer of the human scene. It has a vision of life surpassing any other and is capable of carrying out that vision in a wide variety of ways. It adds depth and passion and dimension to the whole business of living and recovers something of that joy which is the primitive inheritance of the human race. It is based upon and rooted in a personal friendship with God, and this friendship with God is the backbone and *magna carta* of the whole of human life, and the law of holiness.

From this vision of holiness, every person, whether monk, mechanic or matador can build his own unique pathway to God and can weave from the elements of his own life a rich tapestry of holiness. And nothing that is truly human, let it be repeated, is outside the scope of holiness.

Because holiness is not seen in its true human dimension, the work of holiness has become a rather drab and unexciting affair, a private matter cultivated in secret, having no real bearing upon human existence as a whole. Those areas of life which are most personal and most passionate, those experiences which are basic to human existence as a whole, those decisions and choices which make life most real and embody that which is deepest and most meaningful in human life, remain untouched by it, and exist almost as separate entities in the life of the Christian.

The human being we are trying to bring to God is a solid, bodily being of blood and bones, nerves and sinews, feelings and free choices, intense thought and intense passion, destined for the very Vision of God and working out his destiny by his own actions and free choices. The arts and sciences are the products of our fertile mind. Human civilization is our creation. The works of human genius are our possession and our glory. Holiness must embrace all of this and add a dimension to human life which makes all of these even more meaningful.

Holiness then becomes, not an escape, but a challenge, a challenge which gathers into a marvelous unity every human energy, bringing human beings face to face with God, and opening the whole of human life to His influence.

When this view of holiness touches human sexuality, it gives a breathtaking vision of love and a new understanding of God's intentions for men and women in their sexual nature. The recovery of a true concept of holiness is certainly one of the greatest needs of the modern Church.

True holiness despises nothing in human life. It looks upon all things and sees "that they are good" whether it is the superb achievement of the scientist, the joy of young lovers, or the simple play of children. In choosing his pathway to God, the Christian keeps himself supremely free, belittling no genuine human activity, and choosing his own pathway with intelligent freedom. His dignity as a Christian and his value before God are not based upon his particular vocation or the tools that he uses in shaping his destiny. From genuine holiness comes freedom, intensity of conviction, and a style of life that is forceful, energetic and flexible. Because he despises nothing, the genuinely holy person is versatile and free; because he has a deep respect for everything, his life is constantly enriched by new experiences and new discoveries. He remains fresh and young as a child, yet mature of judgment, capable of decisive action and bold new directions.

Any concept of holiness and of human behavior in relation to God which does not consider the whole spectrum of human activities and every human possibility, will not long hold the attention of educated people; and any concept of holiness which limits holiness to an affair of "the soul" is totally inadequate for a full human life. What is needed, first of all, in encouraging others to holiness, is a profound respect for the human person and a deep reverence for every facet of human life.

II
The Breathtaking Dimensions
of Conjugal Love

The foundation of sex is a kind of aston-
ishment and its beauty is something that even,
and especially, the celibate should understand
and be aware of. God uses the image of sexual
love to express the relationship between Himself and human beings; therefore the reality
and the relationship that is imaged has rich
meaning.

Married sex involves the sharing of a deeply
moving and wondrous experience, the expression of a deep personal love, and the sealing of
a covenant that is personal, passionate and
permanent. It involves, by God's creative act,
the complete physical union of a man and a
woman, the communion of two human beings in a ritual of great power and beauty, and
an erotic encounter that is the finest and most
genuine expression of our total humanity. The
wonder, the joy and the ecstasy of sex is the
meeting-place of two lovers who bestow on
each other a freedom, a tenderness and a sense
of well-being unattainable in any other human
experience, bringing to flower a friendship
and a relationship that binds them to each
other in "one flesh", one life, one breath, one
affection.

This interpenetration and constant com-
mingling of their total personalities symbolizes
their total gift of themselves to each other, giv-

ing them a power and a passion for living that is continually renewed, and providing a center of gravity for their existence which strikes at the very roots of their being.

Sexual love is brilliant and shattering, a thunderclap of dazzling power that undermines the monotony and routine that must ultimately creep into any relationship.

Apart from its depth, sex possesses an extraordinary intimacy. Every disclosure of sex is the revelation of something intimate and personal; it is the initiation of another into one's secret. In a sense, sex is the secret of each individual . . . It is the voice from the depths, the utterance of something central and of the utmost significance.

The theologian reverently handles the elements of this intimate communion, knowing that they have been planted in human nature by a divine genius. Nothing in sex is unworthy of human beings, from the root physical contours of the bodily embrace to the deep-seated flood of ecstatic joy that accompanies physical union. Man and woman, in all their sexual reality, are the work of God.

This intimate union[1] which is one of God's greatest gifts to human beings, exists to enliven, deepen and strengthen the love of man and woman in marriage, and to make them, in the profound words of Holy Scripture "two in one flesh", lovers in the deepest sense of the word, constantly finding joy in each other's company.

It is this union[2] that is at the heart of the marriage relationship, the foundation and the binding tie of the marriage covenant. There is boldness and an exquisite beauty to sexual union that is lacking in every other human relationship, for it involves the whole person, on every level of his or her being.

Nor is this union, and the friendship it nourishes, in any way an obstacle to deep friendship with God, in spite of the reservations of generations of ascetics. The important effort in sexual experience is not to restrict and devaluate the sexual reality, but to personalize and deepen it, and to realize in the deepest part of one's psychology, the personal commitment of which sex is but a faint sign.[3]

The dialogue of the celibate with sex must not overlook insights into the beauty of the sexual encounter and the shattering brilliance of conjugal intimacy. For the meaningfulness of celibacy itself is to be measured by the grandeur of the gift that the celibate forsakes, and the scope and style of his own priestly or religious achievements must be at least equal to the energy and joy he would have found in marriage.

Moreover, in the light of this vision of a hallowed sexual companionship, it is evident that the call to celibacy must include a goal and a challenge as breathtakingly beautiful as married love itself, and an achievement equal in its creative capacities as the creative capacities of married love.

The drama of human life is a mirroring of the Beatific Vision which will invade man's being with a matchless joy, opening up to an eternal companionship with God. By the sexual encounter, a man and a woman open their total beings to each other and nourish in tender intimacy a love and a friendship that makes them one heart and soul, and it makes them one in their sexual embrace.

Their quivering flesh becomes the sacrament and sign of a love that is vibrant, passionate and deeply personal, and the cultivation of this love in the secret sanctuary of sex is the first task and most important concern in their lives.

It is true that often marriage does not become that deep and tender companionship that it was intended to be, but part of the blame for this can be placed upon the theologian who has neglected to explore this most basic of human experiences.

God has created human beings for beatitude and the beatitude of married friendship is as valid a path to Him as the more subtle pathway of the celibate. When two people, deeply in love with each other and also deeply in love with God, conscious of their eternal destiny and of their dignity before Him, encounter each other in the intimacy of married friendship, their lives are enriched beyond the wildest conception, and they glimpse in a way that can scarcely be measured, the depths and the wonder of a Divine friendship. In wholesome innocence and in the childlike acceptance of their total physical beings, they mutually explore each other's diversity and know a joy that strikes at the very roots of their being. They are caught up in a drama that is repeated again and again, and, if they are truly lovers, they constantly discover new depths in their relationship that enchants and awes them as they grow in their love.

Often, it is true, love in marriage does not grow in this way, but again this is frequently because the theologian has not helped married Christians integrate sex into their relationship with God, so that those moments which are most personal and most passionate are not brought into the orbit of one's relationship with God. Once a person knows that God is the author of sex in all its naked reality, that He is the architect and molder of the human person, then sex becomes, not only the married couple's bond with each other, but their bond with God and a source of sacred and sanctifying joy.

It is the task of the theologian to delineate the stunning beauty of the sexual encounter and the shattering loveliness of conjugal intimacy. The words of *Gaudium et Spes,* the *Pastoral Constitution on the Church in the Modern World* of the Second Vatican Council have opened a whole new era in the theology of sex and marriage. It marks a unique point in the development of Catholic theology and is the starting point of a totally new theology of sexual love:

The Biblical word of God several times urges the betrothed and the married to nourish and develop their wedlock by pure conjugal love and undivided affection . . . This love is eminently human since it is directed from one person to another through the affection of the will. It involves the good of the whole person.

Therefore it can enrich the expressions of the body and mind with unique dignity, ennobling these expressions as a special ingredient and sign of the friendship distinctive of marriage . . . This love is uniquely expressed and perfected through the marital act.

The actions within marriage by which the couple are united, intimately and chastely, are noble and worthy ones. Expressed in a manner truly human, these actions signify and promote that mutual self-giving which couples enrich each other with a joyful and grateful goodwill.[4]

The choice of celibacy must be seen against the background of this concept of sexual love. Only then does the depth, the power and the magnificence of the celibate's consecration begin to be seen. His consecration to celibacy is not based on the mere absence of sex in his life; it is based upon a consecration to a dimension as personal, as valid, as breathtaking and as absorbing as the sexual consecration of marriage. The absence of conjugal sex in his life is but one item in the totality of his consecration, much as the absence of another woman in the life of a married man is only a negative factor in the full drama of married friendship.

Celibacy is not in itself more generous or more self-sacrificing than the sexual surrender of man and woman in marriage; it is simply one step in a life that is creatively consecrated to a particular intimacy with God and a lifestyle that flows from this. It has neither a universal validity nor a universal usefulness and therefore should be the result of a personal, pragmatic choice. When chosen, it does bear witness to a dimension beyond the human, a dimension which is basic to every Christian life, and is the substratum of human existence itself. Nor is celibacy the only way to bear witness to this dimension. But it is a valid and articulate witness and does have its own peculiar and particular value for the celibate himself and for human civilization. Its value must be seen, however, as complementing and including the values embodied in sexual love.

III
The Celibate Instinct

It is of the very nature of celibacy, as of marriage, to be free from compulsion of any kind. In marrying, a mate is chosen for his or her own sake, from an "instinct" of love; compulsion destroys the very nature of the marriage covenant. It is important for the healthy growth of the vocation to celibacy that what was *implicit* in the choice of celibacy become *explicit* by reflection and personal probing. *Implicit* in the choice of celibacy must be the complete freedom with which the choice is made: that is a complete lack of compulsion of any kind: moral, spiritual, ascetic, especially with regard to celibacy's most obvious counterpart: sexual intimacy in marriage. The older spirituality suggested that celibacy is really better than marriage and in choosing it, you are really being more generous with God; that celibacy is the perfect following of Christ, that it is perfect precisely because of the absence of the sex experience in marriage. The message was that marriage was less perfect than celibacy; that marriage was good, but celibacy was better, because the expression of sex in marriage is less perfect than the total continence of celibacy.

Needless to say, this is a lie, a lie that strikes at the deepest sense of personal identity and worth. But it is a tenet of the older asceticism and is very difficult to eradicate once it has become part of the motivation for celibacy. Perhaps part of the reason for the great exodus of priests and religious from the celibate vocation over the past few years, was the sudden or gradual discovery that this tenet of their spirituality and motivation was a lie and that for the first time in their lives they were free to make a personal choice regarding their "vocation". The whole question of a sound anthropology, one that sees the Spirit of God working *superabundantly* through our own freedom and not delivering moral imperatives making immobile our own personal choice.

Celibacy, too, must be completely free from compulsion and chosen from the same "instinct" of love. One who chooses celibacy is free to marry and, as has been shown, he does not choose celibacy from any sense that sex and married love are unworthy of him. As in choosing a wife, he chooses celibacy for its own sake, drawn by the gift of a particular intimacy with God that it holds out to him, and from an "instinct" of love.

One who chooses celibacy chooses it before he is bound to it, just as a man and woman fall in love before they consecrate themselves to each other by marriage. It is of the very nature of celibacy to be freely chosen with the full realization that marriage and sexual love could be freely chosen as well. Why a person chooses celibacy is as mysterious as why a person chooses a particular man or woman to marry, why he "loves" her, or she him. There is always a personal and private element in the choice of celibacy that cannot be discovered or analyzed, something in the secret depths of the human spirit that is bound up with the nature of love. The celibate has been touched by the beauty and wonder of God in a way that he simply cannot explain. Solitude with God becomes a necessary ingredient of his personal happiness as intimacy with this particular person becomes a necessary ingredient of the happiness of one who marries.

The man or woman who marries does not have to marry this particular woman or man, but freely chooses to do so for the simple reason of love and the desire for an exclusive bond with the beloved. The person who chooses celibacy is perfectly free to marry, but freely chooses celibacy because he is drawn by the wonder of a particular relationship with God. He does not choose celibacy because it is "better"; he does not turn aside from marriage because it is "inferior". In a very real sense, when the definitive choice of celibacy is made, he is as broken with the beauty of God as a married man is broken with the beauty of a particular woman. The pattern is the same, the "instinct" is the same.

The celibate does not pretend that he alone is created for God or that the celibate commitment is the only way to intimacy with Him. Every human being is created for beatitude and the pathways to this beatitude are infinite. Each human being must place his feet on the pathway to eternal life by a definite act of his own, by a free and deliberate decision. The celibate has no secret access to God that is denied to others.

What is important in any choice is not the particular content of that choice but its direction. The celibate has chosen the path of celibacy because this is suitable for him and because it gives him the greatest possible freedom in seeking God and eternal life. Under different circumstances, his choice might have been different, but his choice is based on love and freedom and a profound sense of his dignity before God.

But his celibate pathway does have its own unique qualities and its own unique enrichment. By it, he puts the stamp of his own personality and his own particular "genius" on this particular pathway, much as a married couple put the stamp of their own personalities on their particular marriage. By the fashioning and molding of his celibate life, he fashions and builds his own love-song to God, and in it and by it, he lays hold of God and eternal life. No two love affairs are the same, and no two celibates cultivate their intimate life with God in quite the same way.

His celibate life is a conscious, affective companionship with God which leads to a deep love of and solidarity with other people; just as marriage is a conscious, affective companionship of a man and woman with each other where God is present, guides and blesses it, and which leads to a greater understanding and love of Him and His ways. Husband and wife live in the same house, eat at the same table, sleep in the same bed, inhabit the same rooms, cultivate a deeply private intimacy with each other. You may think that this kind of passion and intimacy is absent from the celibate life. On the contrary, the celibate cultivates a singular intimacy with God with a passion; he dwells in an aloneness inhabited only by God and himself, he experiences something of the massive joy of God. In a very real sense, he has been kissed by God in a way that opens his whole being to God. That is the meaning of the celibate solitude. The celibate works out the deeply private dimension of his life under the aegis of solitude with God. The nature of this private dimension is as inexpressible for the celibate as the singular bond uniting "two in one flesh" is for each married couple.

The celibate chooses the solitude of celibacy as his continual habitat, not because he despises earthly loves or because he has no appreciation for the earthly and the human. "To hold creatures cheaply," writes St. Thomas Aquinas, "is to slight divine power." But it is only in the dimension of celibate personal solitude that he can cultivate his unique intimacy with God with the freedom and intensity that so mysteriously draws him. It is only in this naked solitude that he can hold rendezvous with his Maker. As human lovers need to be alone with each other, he needs to be alone with God. "The lover," writes St. Thomas Aquinas again, "is not content with superficial knowledge of the one loved, but strives for intimate discovery and entrance."

The act of choosing celibacy is essentially an affirmation of the reality of God and the overwhelming reality of eternal life. Like a man in love with a woman, the celibate is willing to put aside every advantage and every other pursuit and activity in order to be with the God Who has won his heart. At the root of the celibate instinct is a thirst for life of incredible magnitude, fed by the realization that the eternal life to which he aspires is "the full and perfect possession of endless life." The celibate's appetite for life is too great for earthly springs to satisfy. His choice of celibacy comes from an exuberance for living that breaks the bonds of the ordinary.

In the original creation, as indicated in the *Book of Genesis*, when Adam saw the woman that God had given him as a gift, his cry of love was a cry of gratitude for the magnitude of the gift and for the marvel of the discovery. The lifestyle of the celibate is likewise a cry of gratitude to God for the gift of being itself, including the gift of his body and the gift of sexuality, and for the gift of eternal life, which is the very possession of God Himself. This cry of gratitude is repeated over and over again, like the intimacies of marriage, as the realization of eternal life dawns on the mind and as the magnitude of the gift impresses itself on the mind through the activity of contemplation.

The celibate life, then, is a special mode of life cultivating a particular total, habitual and intense companionship with God. Like marriage itself, like medicine or jurisprudence, it is simply a specialized form of human life. The married couple, the physician, the lawyer, the artist, the scientist, need their own specialized tools, their own specialized environment and their own special skills to accomplish the purpose of their specialty. So, too, does the celibate. He needs the personal solitude that celibacy provides, an indispensable environment, as critical to him for his intimacy with God as the bridal chamber and the wedding bower are to the bride and groom and to married lovers. St. Thomas has an interesting commentary on this critical need for the celibate to be alone: "The more pursued, the more self-contained it shows itself: that is the prerogative of wisdom. In external works, we rely on the assistance of many others, but with contemplation, we operate more expertly by living alone."[1]

The celibate is not a mystic in a monastery, cultivating a corporate solitude that is apart from the normal concerns and activities of life. Celibacy is also the gift and choice of many others, including diocesan priests and certain lay persons. There are celibates-- monks, nuns, and contemplatives--who live in this kind of solitude, but the personal solitude of celibacy does not require this. Celibacy alone is the solitude; the celibate "sleeps alone"; he fastens his attention and affection

47

on God--breathing, eating, drinking God, in a sense--and sleeping in a subtle, vast and beautiful aloneness where the thought of God can be nurtured. This is the basis of his joy and delight, so profoundly personal, that it can only be hinted at. Again, the insights of Thomas Aquinas:

> Contemplation can be delightful as a function and for its content. The activity is congenial to human nature and instinct, and especially when by it we behold something that we love. Thus, seeing is enjoyable itself, and more so, when we gaze on someone we love dearly.[2]

Let no one say that the celibate's life is devoid of delight or empty of joy!

The one who chooses celibacy does not aspire to be different from anyone else. He does not choose celibacy because he judges it to be "superior" or "more pleasing to God" than marriage. He could just as well go to God on the pathway of marriage, and might have, if he had met the right person at the right time, in the right circumstances. He certainly does not think that intimacy in marriage would have made him any less pleasing to God than his choice of celibacy. He realizes that the option of celibacy was a gift. Celibacy happens to be his pathway, the option he chose, well-suited for him and in keeping with his own desires.

The most important fact about the celibate life is that it is not a bondage but a way of freedom, it is chosen in freedom, and this is a key to its exhilarating joy. Other paths that are chosen with the same freedom and same sense of dignity before God lead to the same exhilarating joy. The celibate life has its own attraction and its own peculiar nourishment, but it is not the only pathway to God. However, it is the celibate's own and becomes for him a wide sky to fly in and a huge continent to explore.

Sometimes the passion of expectation puts itself into words, and then we have poetry, or something resembling that, which tries to approximate in words something of the longing and hunger in the heart:

Oh, I could go, yes, if I wanted to
To some small island off
the shores of Greece
Where rock and bird, and sea and sky,
and pounding surf
Could be my solitude,
And where the vast expanse
Of centuries, reaching backward,
would give me Company enough
for any man.

I could live alone there, and die alone there,
Companion only to the cryptic pedagogy
of sea and sky,
The elemental fabric of existence,
And there unbare in quivering intimacy
That primitive face that's shown
only to God

To tap the primal mother-lode
of my existence
And unashamedly become
The raw recruit of God's devouring splendor.
Perhaps there in that awe-full solitude
I could await the flurry of those wings,
Unhindered in my lasered contemplation,
The flaming flurry of those wings
When galaxies of suns will tear away
The fragile walls of my mortality.

Until that moment, then,
I want to live uplifted to His gaze,
My spirit flexed for utterness,
On some lone island off the shores of Greece,
Or some small place upon this planet
Where only little wild things live,
And where the mountains thunder
out His Name,
And rivet in my unlocked mind and spirit
The *bereshith* of my beginnings,
The cryptic mathematics of His Presence.

IV
Celibate Solitude

The celibate's life demands a regualar portion of solitude. This solitude is the most fundamental skill that he must acquire. Celibacy provides him with a personal solitude and this is indeed the matrix of the celibate life. It is out of this personal solitude that he lives, that he thinks, that he labors, that he seeks God. The solitude does not exist for its own sake, but only to provide him with an environment where intimacy with God can be cultivated with something resembling passion.

In this the celibate is not unlike the married person. Marriage provides a common life for a man and woman, a common life in which their intimacy can be cultivated and experienced. A married couple "lives alone"; they leave father and mother so that they can cleave to each other and become "one flesh". Without this common life, that married solitude, that which is deepest and most meaningful in their relationship, would be impossible or greatly hindered. The personal solitude of celibacy gives the celibate a "common life" with God where intimacy can be cultivated.

But it should be evident that he is not alone; he cultivates an intimacy beyond the power of words to tell. The theological truth behind the life of celibacy is that human beings are created for beatitude, for full and total happiness, for the full and overflowing possession of the very life of God. Everything earthly and human somehow mirrors the reality of eternal life and everything in creation is touched by the beauty of God and reflects something of His greatness and His being. Marriage and human love are one of the loveliest expressions of His goodness, and the beatitude of married love is a true anticipation of that final beatitude. The celibate does not empty his life of marriage and the love for another as the first act in taking on a life of celibacy: this is a reflex act. He takes a step first and primarily towards the joy he feels at the prospect of intimacy with God

It is important to emphasize this aspect of celibacy, for there is no hint in true celibacy of a low judgment of married friendship or any negative attitude towards married beatitude. But the sacrifice of married happiness is no less for all that, and the significance of this sacrifice should not be underestimated. The celibate deprives himself of the crowning act of his natural self. If that terrifying vacuum were not filled with something that struck with joy at his very roots, the deprivation and emptiness would be almost too much to bear. This is a consequence of celibacy that has not often been touched upon, but it certainly explains some of the strange aberrations in clerical and religious life and some of the tragic consequences of an ill-motivated and immature commitment to celibacy.

And that is why the comparison of the solitude in celibacy with that of the life in common of husband and wife is very apt. A common life simply provides a man and woman with that personal and mutual solitude where their intimacy can be cultivated and shared; it does not exist for its own sake. The solitude of celibacy likewise does not exist for its own sake. If that solitude does not lead to the cultivation of intimacy with God, it can become an empty and sterile solitude. The solitude of celibacy must be filled with God and part of the artistry of celibacy is precisely the filling of that solitude with God.

For the celibate, of course, this solitude is more than just being alone. It is freedom in the highest degree. It is a high sky to fly in, a huge wilderness to explore, it is a return to radical simplicity, and the acquiring of a whole new set of instincts and habits.

The solitary dimension of life can be harrowing and pitifully lonesome, because of the human emptiness and the lack of intimate companionship. But it can also be tremendously exciting as new horizons with God are glimpsed and as the marvel and wonder of God become more real and more intimately experienced. Celibates, since they are basically contemplatives, have always had a passion for solitude, and this solitude becomes the symbol and the crown of their celibate consecration, so that solitude with God becomes the very breath of life for them.

In the mutual solitude of marriage, the couple turn towards each other, they begin to unveil and reveal to each other a secret face and a private self that they will reveal to no one else. They begin to cultivate an intimacy with each other that is the very foundation of their relationship and is the living embodiment of their attraction for each other.

In the solitude of celibacy, the celibate turns towards God and opens all his being to God's splendor. He begins the cultivation of an intimacy that is the root reason for his existence. But the solitude itself does not provide this; it merely provides the opportunity.

And there is another aspect to this solitude: it is created by the celibate himself.

Just as in marriage, the fact of marriage itself does not provide a common life for the couple. They have to make plans for the future, find a house for themselves where they can be alone, where they can "set up housekeeping", and fill that house with all the elements of proprietorship and privacy that make it truly their own, that make it suitable for them to live in and inhabit. It must be hugely personal and hugely private, and their very desire to live together and cultivate their love for each other makes setting up a home a very exciting business.

The celibate, too, if his celibacy is genuine, wants to create the conditions where he can live in the Presence of God, turning his face more and more to the God of his being, unbaring to Him, like a bridegroom to his bride, that primitive face and that primitive self that is shown only to God. No one objects that the scientist needs his laboratory, the artist his studio, the musician his conservatory, even the child his playground. Every art and specialty, every skill and pursuit needs its appropriate environment or this particular art, that particular skill, simply cannot be cultivated. The artist without his studio, the scientist without his laboratory simply could not do their work, could not create their works of beauty or their works of the mind, and the human race would be impoverished in consequence. Their work proceeds from a certain kind of "intimacy" and without it, the world is deprived of beauty or of insight.

The celibate needs his solitude, but it must be a solitude that is his own larger world, where the tools and the nourishment for his intimacy with God give him his own unique "culture", his own vast "civilization" where he breathes a different kind of air and sings a different kind of song. And the windows of that culture, that *ecos,* must open onto eternity so that he can keep his face continually against the windowpane of God.

He needs enrichment for his spirit, he needs instruments of joy, he needs worlds to walk into for the cultivation of his mind and the expansion of his spirit. Even a man and wife do not inhabit an empty cottage. If they are wise, they have a marriage bower that never loses the character of the bridal chamber, it has something that encourages the kind of intimacy that is experienced there. It is interesting how the ancient weddings were celebrated, hinted at in historical background of the *Song of Songs*. A nuptial bower was prepared for the couple where they could be alone for their intimacy, a thing of beauty in keeping with their festive mood. It was there that the full unveiling of their love for each other took place. An *ecos* had been created for their intimacy.

It is not enough to be alone: that aloneness must be filled. The filling of that aloneness with the tools for his craft and the nourishment of his mind and spirit is one of the most exciting things about being a celibate. There is a primitive kind of joy in filling spaces with things that reflect your own inner world, the world of your personal history of which you are the product.

It is this kind of habitation of the spirit that the celibate priest has to create: where insight abounds, where intuition is sparked, where ideas flourish and where breathing spaces for the spirit are to be found. First and foremost, the priest must begin to inhabit those awe-filled solitudes where prophets, priests and poets meet their God and sense this ultimate yearning in the world around them.

V
Comitatus Cum Deo

As these pages have tried to show, there is a new theology of celibacy trying to be born, one which is not based on a denigration of sexual love in marriage or on a conflict between the "flesh" and the "spirit" in the spiritual life. It is based rather on a profound respect and appreciation for human sexuality and its expression in conjugal love, and is seen as an affirmation of personal realities that transcend, but are not incompatible with, the sexual. Sexual physical union is excluded from the celibate commitment, not because it is in any way unworthy of the celibate or not in keeping with a total love of God, but simply because the celibate has other plans.

Celibacy is seen as an alternate pathway to God, not as superior to marriage. The celibate, merely because of chastity, does not have some access to God that is denied other human beings. Celibacy is as valid a pathway to God as marriage, but it is not viewed as superior in itself. A choice of celibacy is completely compatible with a profound appreciation for sexual intimacy in marriage and for the gift of conjugal love. The celibate simply chooses another pathway.

But that pathway has its own characteristics and its own splendor and its own unique joys. The celibate pathway is part of the adventure of knowing God, an adventure fully as exciting for a man as knowing a woman, and it reaches out to an intimacy with God that shatters his whole existence and opens his being to the splendor and magnificence of God. In his solitude, the celibate becomes conscious of a love as overwhelming as the love of a man and woman and one that strikes at the very roots of his existence.

In his solitude, he must grapple with the strange equations that are riveted into the very substance of his being, and he must translate and interpret to himself an identity more mysterious than sexual identity and more astonishing than sexual intimacy. If a bridegroom in the presence of his bride is shaken by a wonder and a joy that gives meaning and expression to his total masculinity, a man in the presence of his God is shaken to the very depths by an even more astonishing encounter, and an even more primitive identity.

In trying to explain it, we have to use sexual imagery, for we know nothing more personal or more primitive than that. But it is beyond the sexual and beyond the earthly and it resembles the sexual only in that it is mutual, passionate and leads to an intimacy for which we have absolutely no comparison.

One of the finest expressions of that intimacy was penned by Gerard Manley Hopkins in the opening lines of *The Wreck of the Deutschland*, a remarkable poem on this very encounter with God. Hopkins strikes some of the deep chords of this searing experience and communicates something of the naked wonderment of this elemental confrontation:

> Thou mastering me
> God! giver of breath and bread;
> World's strand, sway of the sea;
> Lord of living and dead;
> Thou hast bound bones and veins in me,
> fastened me flesh,
> And after it almost unmade,
> what with dread thy doing;
> and dost thou touch me afresh?
> Over again I feel thy finger and find thee.[1]

The beginning of this intimacy is awesome, because of the very nature of the relationship. One is facing the God Who made him, Who fashioned his flesh and his bones and his sinews and brought him naked from his mother's womb. There is a primitive awe about encountering the God of your being and realizing that He has given you the very gift of existence, that you are bound to Him by something more than goodwill and good intention. You have been shaped in all your physical reality, in all the depths of your feelings and the liveliness of your senses by this God Who hovers over you in the wonder of the universe.

In the immensity of solitude, somehow, somewhere, the door opens and the invitation is clear. The call to an intimacy so profound and so wondrous that everything in your life up to that moment seems like a far off yesterday. Purely and simply, it is falling in love with God and it is that which begins to fill the solitude. Any priest worthy of the name has been touched by this sometime and it is a golden moment never to be forgotten. But the *cultivation* of this, and that this is the very heart of celibacy, is the soul-searing fact of the very vocation. Celibacy under any other title doesn't make any sense. In very truth, without this profound intimacy, it simply isn't worth it.

What is clear and what makes the moment golden is that you are profoundly loved. This is the solution to almost every personal and spiritual problem. You are loved to the marrow of your bones and it is no longer merely the *belief* in the love of a Father and Creator; it is something more intimate and more mysterious than that. It is a reality, an experience, something totally and massively unexplainable in ordinary terms. It is more like the love of the bride for the bridegroom--at least that is the closest image we have-- God comes in this intimacy purely and simply as a lover and there is no other response except a love and a joy that shatters the depths of your consciousness and brings you face to face with an immense awe. You are cherished in an inexpressible way, in a startling way, that is the beginning of all joy.

The word "love" is scarcely adequate for that massive passion, which St. Thomas Aquinas tried to record with his stylus of steel and fire. How do you relate to something so elemental and so vast, something that reveals a mind and a being of that magnitude and yet a lover of such overpowering beauty; his greatness etched in mountains and in your own living flesh? . . .

> Does he not see and is His gaze not bent
> Upon, the seeker?
> He Who fills the world,
> Whom the stars from nothingness
> were hurled,
> And hurtling still, He holds them.
> Yea, God, Who made with might those veins
> Upon the violet,
> Who hew the mounts and plains
> To what they be, He is a sojourner
> With loneliness, He lives.
> Loneliness is His dwelling-place,
> He lives alone,
> And those who live alone find Him there.

What is strange and incredible and mountainous to the mind is the love that echoes from the other side: the splendid passion of that Godhead, to be loved that way by the Living God.

Then you want to create a solitude where you can live in the Presence of that God, quivering with joy and turning your face more and more to that vast solitude where He dwells, unbaring to Him like a bridegroom to his bride.

But where can such a solitude be found? Every place and every aspect of life is measured by something *less* than that. You have to live in an aloneness, and this is the key to the vocation to celibacy: you need a solitude where you can raise your mind to Him habitually, unhindered, and this can be done only in the most personal solitude.

What the celibate learns is that it must be done alone. No one can walk that awe-filled solitude with you; you have to create your own solitude to live with Him, find places for intimacy with Him, meet with Him in moments of hushed silence and love Him passionately in the depths of your own spirit and in the depths of your own solitude . . . open your eyes to Him, lift your face to His Presence, and dwell in the company of that *Jahwe Ineffabilis*

Celibacy is simply the first step in creating this kind of solitude. There is no other motive for the celibate life than this.

Thus Aquinas:

> God is not confined in time, for He is eternal and without beginning or end. His being is constant, ever present, never altering from past to future. Nothing can be taken away from Him, nothing added, and His Name is *Jahwe Ineffabilis.* He Who is His grandeur exceeds incomparably anything we can know, for He is boundless.[3]

> To realize that God is far beyond anything we can think, that is the mind's achievement.[4]

> God is worshipped in silence; not that we can think or say nothing about him, but that we

should appreciate how far He surpasses our comprehension.[5]

The celibate life is a kind of holiday.[6]

The celibate's experience of intimacy with God is not exclusive with himself nor is it something that is uniquely his own. This intimacy is the inheritance of every human being and is simply a foretaste of the eternal life to which everyone is called. Because of the intensity of his solitude and the total freedom of his lifestyle, his experience has a certain "quality" about it, but that intimacy does not make his way of life "superior", or outside the "common" path of holiness. His opportunity for "savoring" this intimacy may be greater than others, but that is the very reason for the personal solitude of celibacy and the main attraction of the celibate vocation.

The vocation to celibacy needs a mode of life which is designed to contain and foster intimacy with God on a continual basis: its own "ecology", its own setting, its own *ecos*. Intimacy with God has all the intimacy and fragility of the sexual act but it needs a surer privacy, a vaster solitude, a more stable freedom than its humbler counterpart. A celibate is a lover and he seeks a rendezvous with His Maker, with the God of his being, fully as meaningful and fully as wondrous as the intimacies of sexual love, but the preliminaries must be cultivated with as much artistry as the preliminaries of human love-making.

The cultivation of the solitude of celibacy aims first of all at the cultivation of a wide and expansive freedom, a delicious freedom where God is sought and savored continually. The artistry that is needed for this constitutes the particular lifestyle of the celibate. Horizons must be broadened, well-springs dug, and freedom must become the very base from which one works.

The cultivation of this freedom and this solitude is the living of a real and intense companionship with God, the growth of an awareness of eternity, and the exercise of those habits and that artistry which opens one's mind and spirit and consciousness continually to God. The celibate weaves a web of genuine solitude and aloneness around his or her whole life and person, and fills that solitude with those activities and events and symbolic elements that keep his mind and his spirit open to God. He brings with him into that solitude the tools the artifacts, the symbols of his own search for God, those companions of his mind and spirit that have enriched his solitude and journey thus far. His solitude is a sanctuary, an oasis of thought, prayer, study, leisure in God and an intimacy that keeps his whole being in a state of startled wonderment.

The celibate lives in the light of eternity, he measures his life and his convictions by it. It is the "form", the substance, the heart, the "ecology" by which and in which he lives. It is not so much that he has death staring him in the face, as it is that he lives by something beyond death. In a sense, he is deathless, psychologically, since he lives by those realities that are deathless.

To the so-called "practical" man, he is "impractical" and "idealistic", since he refuses to measure his vision or his desires by the "practical" realities of life. But actually, he is the most practical since the realities that the "practical" man lives by will disappear in a very short time.

The celibate bears witness in his own person to the root realities of the Christian Faith which are timeless, and cultivates by intensity of life that companionship with God, the *comitatus cum Deo*, which is the heart of the Christian covenant.

The "practical" person does not think this is possible, or at least does not think it is practical. One's life, in this view, should be measured by the practical demands and necessities of everyday life and anything else is an escape and a luxury. Actually, the practical man's life is an escape from taking seriously the larger dimension, and his so-called practicality will end with death.

The celibate measures his life, his hope, his desire, his pre-occupation, his activities, his study, the thrust of his whole existence by the eternal and permanent. His refusal to measure his life by anything else is a refusal to be a partial man. He certainly lives with the realities and fabric of a day to day existence, and is deeply interested in his times, his contemporaries and the human situation in which he has to live. But he refuses to measure his life by these and in the long run is the only one who can be at home anywhere, at anytime, with anyone.

He is the inhabitant of larger world. He measures his life by something which does not end with death.

Thus, theology is his passion, liturgy his joy, prayer his natural habitat. His life more and more takes on the form of his theological vision, the form of the eternal. His life, psychically and emotionally, is a continuum with eternity itself. And those who live by other visions and measure their lives by other realities find him an enigma and a puzzle. He, on the other hand, is not aware of being different from anyone else, since he lives by a vision that is common to all, or at least is the common heritage of all.

Everything he touches sharpens that vision and nourishes that thrust towards the eternal, everything he touches deepens his companionship with God and nourishes that passion for His Presence. His continuum with the eternal grows stronger with every step he takes for it is the measurement of everything he is and everything he does.

The celibate's life and expectations are measured by something beyond the grave and his expectations grow as the vision of eternal life becomes sharper and deeper.

VI
Sacramentum Tremendum

> Sudden as wind that breaks east out of dawn
> this morning you struck,
> As wind that poured from the wound of the
> dawn in the valley of my beginning.
> Your look rang like the strident quail, like the
> buck that stamps in the thicket.
> Your face was the flame. Your mouth the rinse
> of wine. Your tongue, the torrent.[1]

How is it possible to express the intimacy with God that we experience in the Eucharist? This moment of intimacy is the culmination of longing for God and the very crown of the celibate condition. It is the final goal of his "aloneness" when his mind and his spirit touch something of eternity and God enfolds him in the very garment of immortality.

The destiny of every human being is an intimacy with God in this life and, in eternity, a matchless existence with God Himself. In the Eucharist the priest touches upon that destiny in a special way and meets in a conclave with the God Who created him. There is nothing like this intimacy in the whole of human existence and the human mind and human words can only tremble in the presence of so awesome an encounter.

The center and focal-point of existence for a celibate is this intimacy with God, and, if he reflects at all, he will admit that this intimacy was what he craved from the first moment that the thought of priestly or religious life dawned on him. From that first moment, the Eucharist beckoned to an intimacy that shattered his whole existence and opened his whole being to the splendor and magnificence of God.

No one can even faintly begin to understand the vocation to celibacy unless he understands this, just as no one can understand the vocation to marriage unless he understands the shattering significance of sexual intimacy. The celibate is not without intimacy and not without joy, but it is an intimacy with God and it is a joy that gives him a share in the very happiness of God.

The reality that must be brought into focus in pondering the Eucharist for all Christians is the reality of God's closeness, the reality of a relationship so rich and so meaningful that God fashions new and astonishing ways to bring human beings into intimacy with Him. With the Eucharist, the celibate returns somewhat to the breathtaking wonder of his original creation, when Adam walked with God and knew the wonder and joy of a Divine Friendship. In the Eucharist, God comes into his very being and the thundering reality of His presence gives to his life a meaning and a stability that he can get from no other source.

Moreover, He comes as a lover, to give His lovers a share in His own happiness. Just as surely as the intimacy of man and woman in marriage is the setting and the source of the indescribable joy they have in each other and the inexhaustible fountain of their own happiness, the Eucharist is the setting and source of the happiness of the religious who enters into a wondrous intimacy with his Creator and begins to share in the very happiness of God. The same Eucharistic experience holds true, of course, for the married person, just as it is also true that the celibate can enjoy certain kinds of intimacy with other people. The distinction boils down to a balance of portion between the Eucharist on the one hand, and and human relationships on the other, which each Christian, married or celibate, chooses to depend upon in order to grow in love. But along with each of these two choices come deep implications which mold our life accordingly. The celibate's life and his experiences are simply not the same as they would have been had the celibate chosen marriage instead.

Down before so deep a Mystery, wrote St. Thomas Aquinas, *Let our beings lowly bow*, not just for the sake of awestruck adoration, but in recognition of our identity. The sense of identity that the Eucharist gives stabilizes human life and gives it a strength and significance surpassing any philosophy or any role one may play in human affairs. Our sense of our own value does not come from what we do or where we labor, but from what we are. Whether we are president or peasant neither adds nor takes away from our essential value. Our relationship with God and with an eternal destiny, which the Eucharist strengthens and deepens, is the abiding reality and this encounter with God in the Eucharist brings down upon the human being the full weight of his true significance.

The God Who is poised above the universe as its Creator and Maker is poised likewise like an eagle above each individual human being. With more power than a whirlwind and with all the rich generosity of His Godhead, He comes into our being in the Eucharist and, with the sharp flame of His Spirit, plants His seal upon our very person.

The human and theological dimensions of the Eucharist reach out to the borders of human history and beyond them. They extend to whatever limit human beings can go with their God-given genius and then reach out even more to more distant horizons. The works of God, of which the Eucharist is the mightiest, are not meant to belittle the labor and effort of human genius, but to make human beings in their labors conscious of the God and the destiny which called them into being.

> Almighty God comes
> creation's God, man's maker.
> Now must my thoughts dwell on deeps,
> render asunder the shell of things,
> and gazing through the bread see God,
> and seeing God,
> let fall the curtains of my thoughts,
> and dwell with God Who comes to me.
> For Christ comes, and all creations' doors

swing back, and all eternal bells ring out:
"Hosanna, alleluia, Lord!"
The thanes in hell   in horror stop
and feel the thunder of His Godhead.
And burning spirits beings bend
before a Mystery so deep.
The culmination of creation,
substance of our ancient faith,
nourishment of Christ's redeemed ones:
bread that is flesh, and flesh that is God.

At the beginning of my studies, the reality of the Eucharist began to emerge as the center of my priestly existence. For me, it was never merely a ritual or a mere belief, or the distinctive action of the priest. Purely and simply, the Eucharist was God, and I bent in adoration before this overpowering Presence that I could neither fathom nor explain. From my first days of study, it had filled me with a delirious joy that stabilized my whole existence and left me in awe of a God Who almost seemed to hold me in his grasp.

The Eucharist in very truth was the point of intimacy, and that was the root reason why I had become a celibate and a priest. The sense of wonder that I felt in its Presence is something that has never left me. Moreover, it is something that has grown with the years and I am thrilled to the depths of my being each time I stand at that altar and hold this mystic rendezvous with my God.

During these early days, there was simply a deepening of all this. The priesthood and the consummation of this intimacy was dead ahead, and I knew that within the solitude of the priesthood, I could be alone with God as I waited for the dawning of that closeness to God that I wanted so desperately. But now I could exult in it, find joy in it, root myself in it, and look forward to the fullness of this intimacy when the doors of the priesthood finally opened wide for me.[2]

The Eucharist is the very heart and center of any Christian's intimacy with God, and for the celibate, it is the heart and center of intimacy itself; not only the center, but the intense furnace of his affective life and the laserpoint of his whole existence. The experience of the Eucharist is the living source of the indescribable joy that shakes his being to its very depths and keeps him conscious continually of the magnitude of God.

Nor is this intimacy limited to the celibate. It is the living patrimony of every human being and is the living pledge of God's overpowering love for each individual human being. The celibate is simply closer to the flame, in a sense, by his very life-style, but the intimacy that the Eucharist fosters is not unique to him and it is possible for even him to be untouched by its earthshaking significance.

In 1976, friends in Santa Fe invited me to take a trip to Mexico City and I went along as a sort of chaplain. Our last evening in Mexico found us at the *Ballet Folklorico de Mexico*, perhaps the most amazing piece of entertainment I have seen in my lifetime. This whole choreographic masterpiece is the history of

Mexico in dance, with a depth and variety and sheer elegance of performance that is unmatched anywhere. In the middle of the program was a carefully chiseled dance drama that struck me with all the force of a small earthquake.

It was the Dance of the Deer. A young dancer, stripped to the waist, wearing Indian gear, a deer head and antlers mounted on his head, gripping hooves in his hands, enters an empty stage, simulating the prance of the deer. To his left and rear, two symbolic hunters emerge with bows and arrows in their hands and the symbolic stalking of the deer begins. The dance is symbolic of one of the Mexican Indian tribes who depend on the deer for their survival, or at least did in ancient times. What the dance celebrates is the death of the deer, for the death of the deer is their very life, their very survival.

In this remarkable piece of choreography, the deer is symbolically stalked, hunted and killed. What struck me was the astonishing similarity to our celebration of the Eucharist in which we celebrate the very death of Christ, which gave us life, and are nourished on His very Body and Blood to bring us into communion with our Maker. I was in awe at the amazing imagery and the graphic portrayal of the *Sacramentum Tremendum* that had taken place before my eyes. I still have the ballet program of that evening, with the young dancer who portrayed the deer on the cover. It is a powerful image of the mystic meaning of that awesome Sacrifice. We *celebrate* the death of Christ. What that meant had never struck me quite so forcefully. To this day I go back to that scene on the cover whenever I want to ponder the Mystery of the Eucharist.

What impressed me was the manner of the celebration: the meaning was enmannered in the act, a powerful example of the priest's role in the celebration of the Eucharist. His manner of celebration reveals and uncovers for himself and those he leads in worship the *mysterium tremendum* that he celebrates. This very manner transforms the consciousness of those for whom he celebrates and every accent of his speech, every flicker of his eyelid betrays an inner being awestruck in adoration. By his manner, the priest moves on the threshold of another world, the immensity momentarily engulfs the time and place of worship.

It is this mystic communion with his God and his openness to savor the full meaning of what he encounters that transforms the very person of an individual and shatters his consciousness with an awareness of the Living God. If he really gets close to that flame, that furnace of being, something of its marvel and wonder rubs off on his person and roots him in a joy he could not possibly conceal. In the celebration of the Eucharist, his intimacy with God is realized and gives him a foretaste and an intimation of what God has in store for those who love him.

In my heart you were might.
And thy word was the running of rain
That rinses October.
And the sweetwater spring
in the rock.
And the brook in the crevice.
There is nothing known like this wound,
this knowledge of love.
In what love? In which wounds, such words?
In whose touch?
In whose coming?[3]

VII
The Season of Glad Songs

By his very person, the celibate is a bearer of glad tidings, the kind of glad tidings that have been translated into every nerve and fiber of his being and shout to the world through the look in his eye and the joy in his life. The kind of joy that comes from deep intimacy with God.

This has nothing to do with "sanctity" in the old sense of superb ascetic mastery and a flawless moral perfection. It is more like the joy that children have on Christmas morning or lovers in each others presence.

Josef Pieper, in *LEISURE the Basis of Culture* speaks of the deep roots of this joy, something he calls "leisure", but which is really a very ancient word for finding joy in God and in His universe:

> Leisure is possible only on the premise that a man consents to his own true nature and abides in accord with the mean of the universe . . . Leisure draws its vitality from affirmation. It is not the same as non-activity, nor is it identical with tranquillity; it is not even the same as inward tranquillity. Rather, it is like the tranquil silence of lovers, which draws its strength from concord.[1]

What the celibate breathes, from the depths of his celibate solitude, is a happiness for which there is no visible or discernible source. And it is this happiness that he shares in every act of his religious life, every work and event that he puts his hand to. This, certainly, is the main result of the cultivation of intimacy with God, "so much in love with all that I survey" (--St. Francis).

If we have not understood this, we have not understood the vocation to celibacy. Celibacy does not give up joy, it takes it in huge gulps. The celibate does not exchange the joys of physical intimacy for intimacy with God. Intimacy with God is as much a part of his human heritage as sexual intimacy. He has simply made this his special province. That is why to say that he "sacrifices" the joys of sex in marriage for some deeper joy is in itself a subtle put-down of the joys of marriage, as if they were some cheap kind of joy, a joy really not in keeping with the spiritual dignity of the celibate.

Both intimacies and *both* joys are his heritage; both are splendid gifts of God and not merely for himself but for the whole human race. Intimacy with God has simply become such a passion of his life that he chooses to concentrate on this as his life's occupation. Not for one moment does he think that the joys of sex which are an integral part of his nature are beneath his dignity. He is perfectly comfortable with his own sexuality and with its wondrous possibilities. He has simply chosen to concentrate on something else.

That is why we will never appeal to the young by telling them that to be a priest or religious they must "sacrifice" the joys of sex in marriage for celibacy, as if sex were some kind of surplus commodity with which God has endowed the human race and the celibate some kind of a superior being who can very well do without it. This kind of thinking has brought nothing but misery to hundreds of priests who made this kind of "sacrifice" because they thought God demanded it of them.

Sexual intimacy is an endowment of God to each individual human being, a personal gift of His goodness, His wisdom and His benevolence. It is a gift denied to no one; it is an integral part of our humanity and our masculinity, and no human power on earth can deprive us of it because it comes with the very blueprint of our nature.

There is no "exchange" in the choice of celibacy; there is simply a concentration on one dimension of one's existence and the cultivation of that dimension as the sole occupation of one's life. In the celibate, the intensity of that passionate pre-occupation overflows in an amazing variety of ways, to make fertile the lives of others and to enrich them with the treasures that he himself possesses.

In the opening lines of his Inaugural Lecture St. Thomas quotes the Psalmist: *You have watered the hills from your upper rooms; the earth shall be filled with the fruit of Your work,* describing the work of the priesthood in the world; he continues:

> . . . as the mists and waters fall upon high mountains, unite, and break and tumble through a thousand rents and fissures, working their way down, forcing their way on, till they reach the broad plain, clothing it with fruitfulness, nourishing the wild life there, sprouting tree and grain and flowers, so the stream of Truth, blending with a man's mind and substance, clothes him with strength and dignity (--from Aquinas' *Principium*).

The root and burning center of the celibate's own effectiveness and creative fruitfulness is his own intimacy with God. It is this intense center of the celibate existence that has sparked creative genius from the very beginnings of Christianity: from the Scriptural genius of Origen to the mystical-pastoral genius of St. Basil of Caesarea; from the contemplative genius of St. Cuthbert of Lindisfarne to the missionary genius of St. Boniface; from the cultural genius of Irish monasticism to the social genius of the Jesuit Reductions in Paraguay; from the theological genius of St. Thomas Aquinas to the pastoral genius of Pope John XXIII. There is no limit to the horizons of priesthood and the future will certainly hold for the Church and for the world surprises as monumental and significant as any of the past.

When Father Edward Flanagan began his work with men on the streets of Omaha in

1913, there were no precedents for what he was doing.[2] After a Midwest drought that year, hundreds of men were stranded in Omaha with no money to return home and no place to stay. As an assistant pastor at St. Patrick's Church in Omaha, Father Flanagan saw the need for a special kind of ministry and responded with food tickets, old clothing and, finally, a "Workingmen's Hotel" where the men could find some kind of shelter from the cold. He badgered the St. Vincent de Paul conferences of the city for money and lured his own family into working on special projects for the men.

When the jobless men finally moved on, his "Workingmen's Hotel" became a refuge for tramps, hobos, drunks off the streets and various kinds of vagrants passing through Omaha.

Contrary to his popular image, Father Flanagan was a first-class scholar, educated at Rome and at Innsbruck, Austria. He put his scholarly talents to work on the social problem he faced. After an exhaustive study of 2,000 of the men who passed through the hotel, he saw that most had come from broken homes and broken families; most had begun their purposeless existence when they were boys. "I saw," he wrote later in *The Romance of the Homeless Boy*, "that this waste of lives was preventable."

From time to time his "Workingmen's Hotel" sheltered a few newsboys. The similarity of the boys' home situation and the men's stories was too terrifying for him to overlook. A search for other boys led him to the juvenile courts. Suddenly, unexpectedly, he had five boys on his hands. He found himself torn between two tasks, either of which would take all the time, money and energy he could put into it. Without hesitation, he closed the "Workingmen's Hotel". In another house, in another part of the city, Father Flanagan's Boys Home was born. Today Boys Town is a monument to his creative genius, which flowed from a priestly vision he had acquired in his seminary days.

His application of Christian principles to the concrete circumstances in which he moved and the moral fiber and intellectual insight that he displayed were classical in the best sense of that term. The superb artistry with which he maneuvered his work for boys into the public eye and changed, in a few bold strokes of imagination, the passion and prejudice of a whole generation, suggest something more than conventional priestly piety and Irish wit.

The grain of his personality was a rare balance of humanity, insight and sheer nerve, coupled with an educated innocence that looked human tragedy straight in the face. He had few precedents for his work: he simply followed his Christian and priestly instincts, with a dogged determination that ultimately convinced others. He seems to have recognized early in his priesthood that the future could not be something that he would merely inhabit, but something that he would have to create. It is that creative insight that is the blueprint for priestly work and it was something that he learned early in his priesthood.

The greatest mistake that is made in priestly work is the conviction that the mere management of resources, financial or otherwise, is the key problem and critical burden of the pastoral task. This has never been true. The critical factor in priestly work is the priest's own intimacy with God and it is from this glowing center that everything vital and viable flows.

The pastoral task itself is that "season of glad songs" of the priestly existence, the symphony he composes to the glory of God, flowing from a deep happiness which is the inexhaustible spring of his own priestly genius. For that season to arrive, the very roots of the priest's psychology must be immersed in a happiness that comes from deep intimacy with God. Not to have learned that is to remain a child playing with his toys and never to have known the kiss of God which must be indelibly seared into the living flesh of one's

VIII
The Furnace of Prayer

To speak of prayer in connection with the vocation to celibacy is to talk about something so intimate and so personal that it is best to leave much unsaid. It is the unveiling of the intimacies between a passionate lover and the one he loves. The intimate details of this profound relationship remain hidden--private and secret from the eyes and knowledge of everyone--but it can be talked about in general terms, as we can talk about human love and make sense out of it. Prayer, however, in this sense, is not a science, it is an art and it is acquired only in that intimate communion that each one of us has with our God.

There is a totality to prayer that opens up every room of our personality and every avenue of our existence to the sobering and illuminating gaze of God. I am a definite person, with a past, a history, a blend of qualities and characteristics quite unlike any other. No one has walked my particular path, no one has been shaped by the forces that have shaped my life. My prayer must express and define the particular person that I am, on every horizon of my particular life.

Prayer is an affirmation in the living language of our own inner psychology, of the root realities of your existence. It is more than this, of course, since it is a communion and a companionship with the very giver of existence. But it expresses the root meaning of what it means to exist and what it means to exist as a friend and lover of God.

Ultimately, prayer must come face to face with the root reality of the human condition, the absurdity and peril and extreme fragility of human existence. All human relationships, all human conditions must ultimately end on the human level as we know it. This is the absurdity and this is the peril. And this is the one basic reality that makes most discussion of prayer an exercise in futility.

In prayer, one must come to grips, not only with his own mortality, but also with the elemental fabric of his own existence. That "coming to grips" brings about a tension of opposites, a tension that is the very core of the business of prayer. In *The Wreck of the Deutschland*, Gerard Manley Hopkins describes some of this "coming to grips":

> I did say yes
> O at lightning and lashed rod;
> Thou heardest me truer than tongue confess
> Thy terror, O Christ, O God;
> Thou knowest the walls,
> altar and hour and night;
> The swoon of a heart that the sweep
> And hurl of thee trod
> Hard down with a horror of heights;
> And the midriff astrain with leaning of,
> laced with fire of stress.[1]

Ultimately, we are deceived by the human condition, especially as it becomes institutionalized and gives a kind of psychic certainty of permanence and durability. This is when prayer either tears a man to shreds or sears into his being a dialogue with the unutterable and unearthly. This does not mean in any way that things lose their significance or that we lose our personal bonds with them. Nor does it mean that we despair in the face of the absurdity and peril. It simply qualifies and determines the modality with which we encounter those things and integrate them into our lives. But more important, it qualifies and determines the modality with which we encounter God. It unlocks every corridor of our inner being and enables us to unbare our deepest inner self to God. This is the ravishing power and scathing fury of prayer. And this describes only the process. It says nothing of our own living intimacy with the God of our being, or the hunger of spirit that begins to savor the wonder and the magnitude of God, or the expectations that begin to be glimpsed in that incredible and singular intimacy.

Prayer is a problem because insensitivity to God has become an advanced problem. We have to rediscover the questions to which faith and prayer are the answer. We are faced with the atrophy of the faith-instinct and a massive social and interpersonal breakdown that has lowered human expectations and therefore faith-expectations. The most common counterfeit of prayer is the labored scrutiny of tortured mediocrities, with the chronic refusal to accept a vision of personal and human significance, the chronic refusal to recognize God's active, existential concern for my individual personality, my living, conscious self.

Genuine prayer, because it is a true communion with God, keeps expectations high. It prevents that lowering of expectation that often comes with "experience", the loss of idealism and vision that some look upon as maturity. Only too often, clarity of purpose and forceful living are tempered with time and give way to less intense habits. When human expectations begin to die, so does all true prayer. Mediocrity becomes the norm and anything resembling high expectations are looked upon as unreal. When and how this subtle substitution takes place, it is hard to say, but that it does happen is evident in every phase and on every level of the Christian and religious life.

Prayer is communion and companionship with the Creator of the universe, the Hidden God, the *Jahwe Ineffabilis*, Who calls us to a living, conscious, vibrant intimacy with Him; in faith, but no less real.

Prayer must open to us the fantastic possibilities of this relationship and nourish expectations that are worthy of this God and the revelation He has given us. True prayer cannot leave us static and passive; it bears fruit in a certain kind of spiritual fruitfulness that leans continually upon the integrity of God and educates one to the true dimensions of hope. It is in the white-heat of conflict and struggle that such instincts are born.

Prayer is the common way, the fruit of normal faith and normal intelligence. There is an infinite variety to its expression and a perpetual freshness to its styles. It is something that each person cultivates for himself integrating into his prayer and his relationship with God, the living texture of his own life.

In this sense, it is not common, it is unique for each one. It is common only in the sense that it is part of the heritage of faith that is given to every human being. We are all alike in that we are the individual creation of God and are totally loved by Him; we are unlike in how we cultivate intimacy with Him and how we bring every element of our existence into the orbit of that intimacy.

The best book on prayer I have read recently was not a serious treatise on mysticism or contemplative prayer, still less one of the many remarkable books on Thomas Merton that seem continually to come off the presses. The best book on prayer I have read recently are the three volumes of Clifton Fadiman's *World Treasury of Children's Literature.*[2] Treatises on mysticism are heavy and ponderous and introspective, quite unlike prayer at its best, and books on contemplative prayer are usually so arbitrary in their portrayal of this delightful exercise that they weary the mind. Prayer brings out the child in us, returns us to the springtime of the world and is to the serious business of living the equivalent of play in the lives of children. "In any true man," Fadiman quotes Nietzsche, "hides a child who wants to play."[3]

Fadiman is a true mystic when he reminds children in his introduction to these volumes: "I didn't read to get ahead of anyone else, or to improve marks in school. I read for the same reason we all like to open Christmas gifts. Each book was a surprise package stuffed with things I had no idea ever existed."[4]

There could be no better introduction to prayer than that. If we are going to talk about prayer, we had better start there, with a sense of wonder, rather than with learned treatises on infused contemplation, or the dark night of the soul, or the interior mansions of St. Teresa of Avila.

We start to pray because we are struck by a sense of wonder: the wonder of life itself, the wonder of God's ways with human beings and the wonder that Fadiman himself experienced in the written page: "Here I was, a rather dull boy looking at an unopened book. Then within a short time, the dull boy found that he was entertained, amused, saddened, delighted, mystified, scared, dreamy, puzzled, astonished, held in suspense . . . surprised."[5]

The cultivation of prayer is not insensitivity to or a denial of the weighty problems of the contemporary world or of one's personal history, still less is it a denial of the joy of living or the normal joys of life. It is not a shirking of responsibility in the face of massive human need: it is the affirmation of the final answer to all human need and a tapping of the springs that make life worth living at all.

And that is why Clifton Fadiman is a better guide to what prayer is all about than many others writing about it. He sees the very activity of the mind as something resembling play, and he sees books as great worlds to play in, words as marvelous inventions to surprise and delight us; he sees preoccupation with words as something distinctively human and almost angelic. Since the Christian who prays is one who is constantly preoccupied with "the Word", what better guide to what words are all about than Clifton Fadiman. And words about prayer should always contain something of wonder and something of surprise.

In trying to find out what prayer is all about, we have to take our cue from someone like Clifton Fadiman who has never lost that sense of wonder in the face of the complexities of living and who understands that there is a strange wonderful secret behind the universe and that we are called upon to discover it, to discover it constantly, to discover it again and again, and to rediscover it at every stage of our existence.

In a recent book, Harvey Egan[6] has shown that mystical writers today are more concerned about the "mysticism of the commonplace, of everyday life, of the mysticism of God's love permeating all aspects of human life." There is little or no concern about exalted states of prayer, the psychological states of holy people, or the "active" and "passive" nights with which an older genre of spiritual writing was concerned. Such things are outside the experience and perception of most people. Prayer is seen as the deep personal solitude where the lover seeks the Beloved. It is as simple as that.

What that means to the celibate in his personal solitude of celibacy is as strange and mysterious and as perpetually exciting as any intimacy must be. It is revealed only in the deep happiness that shines out of his eyes and breaks forth a certain kind of deep-seated mirth. It is a secret deep inside him that he can share with no one, the burning center of his existence and the living furnace of his every hope and desire.

IX
God's Devouring Splendor

The celibate needs first of all an artistry of mind.

The artistry of mind is a theological skill and a theological culture, the development of theological knowledge and theological competency, the cultivation of the sanctity of the intellect, the acquiring of the *habitus* of theology.

Pre-occupation with God is the heart of the celibate commitment. He must be charmed, enchanted, delighted, absorbed, awed with God, and he must prepare his mind with a wealth of theological insights to nourish and sustain, to enliven and enrich this pre-occupation! The cultivation of a truly contemplative spirit, nourished by a broad and rich theology, is the first skill of the celibate for it is by this contemplative spirit that he begins to taste the wonder and the magnitude of God.

The pattern of this theological occupation is laid down in a remarkable passage of St. Thomas Aquinas where he lays out the blueprint of this theological culture:

> Since a man's fullness and wholeness consists of intimacy and intimate communion with God it is most proper that with all that is in him and with all the powers of his being, he should penetrate Divine things and be wholly

occupied with them, so that his mind may be absorbed in contemplation and his reasoning powers in the exploration of those things that are of God.[1]

The effect of this theological culture upon the mind of the priest cannot be over-estimated by this kind of theological "exploration". The human mind comes into living, vital contact with the deathless, ageless and timeless God, acquiring, thereby, a stability and a perspective of incredible magnitude and strength. By a strong passion of the mind, the priest acquires the artistry and ability to lean upon the integrity of God and to educate himself to the true dimensions of hope. He is able to develop a wholesome independence in following his own carefully chosen pathway, and yet a deep sense of the freedom and in-dividuality of others. Besides, and this is the critical point, this theological exploration be-gins to reveal, however faintly, the face of God, and the more the face of God is re-vealed, the more He is loved, indeed, the more passionately He is loved.

Moreover, this constant probing and exploration of theological knowledge provides that solitude of spirit and immensity of mind where the seeker of God can tear away the bindings and faces that he shows to others through necessity or convention, to bare his naked being in this intimacy of solitude and unbare that primitive face that is shown only to God. These vast theological wildernesses are shelters for his spirit, spaces for intimacy, intuition and self-revelation, which are the living pulse of prayer.

This kind of theology gives a delicious freedom in living and is the cutting edge of an overpowering kind of prayer and provides the environment for the wildest kind of mirth and the deepest kind of joy.

The most important occupation of the priestly and celibate life is this "exploration" of God. This "theology" and this theological discipline is aimed precisely at preparing the mind and heart of the priest and other celibates for this exploration. The term of this exploration is that blinding moment when the celibate meets God fully and consciously at death; the immediate effect of this exploration is prayer, but not prayer as a passing event or static act, but prayer as a living, consciousness of the Living God, and an intimacy with Him that is beyond human comprehension. This theological exploration makes us perpetually, vibrantly and sometimes ecstatically, conscious of Him.

The vocation to celibacy is shot through with a fantastic irony and a magnificent conceit, and this underlies both its permanency and its tragedy. No celibate can escape from the irony of a Divine permanence bundled into his total personality, nor can he escape the magnificent conceit which is at the very root of his task. This dialectic, this tension between the human equation in celibacy and the alien and untranslatable core that defies all human mathematics is bound up with the very notion of celibacy.

It can be sensed in all its tragic poignancy in the bewildered groping of the ancient Hebrew prophets, scrawling their message from Jahwe in cryptic accents that, in Hebrew, still ring with a finality that tore their beings apart. The soul-searing nature of celibacy carries with it that possibility of immense tragedy and incredible joy and one is marked with a joy that shines through every nerve and sinew of his clumsy self, or by a tragedy that marks him as a burnt angel who dared to fly into the sun.

Men do not write of celibacy the way that lovers write of love, as this study has amply shown. The beauty, the joy and ecstasy of sexual love is marked with a similar joy and a similar tragedy, and lovers can find their role-models in a literary tradition as ancient as the written word itself. It is etched in the first pages of the Book of Genesis, where a subtle but reverent eroticism portrays the dialectic of the man-woman relationship, and in the *Song of Songs*, the full flood of Divine Revelation lifts the veil momentarily on the shattering significance of the sexual encounter.

Celibacy has no such literary tradition and no such role-models, and so the celibate of today, cut off from the cultural roots that gave significance to his vocation in the past, must grapple with the strange equations riveted into the very substance of his being, revealing realities even more elemental than erotic awakening. He must translate and interpret to himself that Divine impress that has seared itself into the very fiber of his being.

The inner word, the *logos*, by which he expresses this to himself is critical to the quality and thrust of his whole religious life.

What is it that mediates meaning to the mind? What event, what omega point catapults the celibate into this encounter with his own self? What is it that scars into his intellect that concept of his identity as earth-shattering and transforming as the sexual awakening of young lovers?

For Thomas Aquinas--in my opinion, the most amazing blend of mind, priest, theologian, contemplative and apostle in the history of the Church--it was the shattering quality of the Greek genius, the analog of reason's possibilities, that opened to his mind the possibilities of redeemed humanity and his own role as priest and theologian. The earthly goal of man itself was so magnificent, he saw, that he had to second-think every fact and feature of his inherited faith. Without this analog, it is quite possible that St. Thomas Aquinas would have remained as conventional and ordinary as other theologians of his day. The analog, it must be insisted, was the fruit of his own thinking and his own intellectual labor.

There are those who would make the crisis of religious vocations today a crisis of faith in the face of a vast spiritual breakdown, when what we are actually faced with is a crisis of reason in the face of a vast cultural change.[2]

In the religious life there is a dialectic that can only be resolved by a living and vibrant concept of the religious life itself. The elements of that concept must be drawn from the living tradition of religious life in the Church, in its many varieties and roles down through the centuries, and expressed in the living language of the mind. Reason must be stirred to grapple with the concrete historical context in which a religious vocation finds itself, and to find new facets in the celibate identity to answer the present need. An equation must be set up to express the blending of the human and the Divine in celibacy and it is quite possible that for each generation there will be a different equation.

The Pauline equation is different from the Petrine equation; the equation of Augustine is different from that of Aquinas; the equation of Cyril and Methodius is different from that of Matteo Ricci; and the equation of the Black Priest in Tanzania will be different from that of the White Priest in Suburbia, U.S.A. Like the local wines of France, Spain and Italy, each expression of religious life will have a different tone and flavor. But all must be shot through with the *madre vino* of the religious life itself. There is a Divine factor in the equation which is common to all.

The inner fabric of the celibate psyche is essentially theological, and somewhere the *esse* and the *ethos* of this psyche must intersect with Revelation, with the whirling and swirling intuitions captured in the Scriptures in human language, penning the lineaments of the theological personality of the human being. The lasered penetrations of the Divine genius must somehow alloy with the basic ore of the human personality, bringing to blossom and to bud a tempestuous logos of rich-kernelled thought. The mind that is not stirred by Revelation must ultimately find a cheaper alloy and history records the watering down of the religious personality in ages as various as 10th century Rome and 17th century France. In both ages, theological science was at a very low ebb.

The religious life swings continuously between Yes and No, between the utter nakedness of the Hebrew prophet before his Lord and the provisioned scribe ready for any good work. The religious, often in his lifetime, will feel the helplessness and hopelessness of his human condition, crying out in anguish in the face of the silence of God, having come to an end of his human mathematics and his human resources. It is as inevitable as the physical decline that comes with old age. Human beings share uncertain lives with rabbits and with pine trees, and the religious is no exception. He must learn, like all Christians, to tense himself for a harvest vaster than his seed. For this he needs, perhaps more than others, the spark-gap of the theological act.

This spark-gap is at once the fruit of his own intellectual effort and a living contact with the Word of God. This does not mean, as is so often stated, a mere "meditative reading" of the Sacred Text, a mere familiarity with the Sacred Writings. It means the intellectual "shattering" of revealed concepts, the systematic "tearing apart" of revealed insights and intuitions, and their re-assimilation into the fabric of his own mind.[3]

His own theological "diggings" are as important to the religious as the diggings of the archeologists are to his profession, and must be done with the same painstaking care. His theological safari must be his own exploration of revealed truth and his own personal discovery of what is for him uncharted territory. In the exploration of theology, no two theological journeys are alike, since each one of us penetrates Divine Truth with his own equivalent of pick and shovel.[4] It is possible that many religious have never known the exhilaration of theological discovery and the transforming experience of the theological act. The tension in the dialectic of religious life can be resolved by nothing else.

Nothing short of a miracle can preserve the celibate psyche from disintegration apart from this "experience" of theology.[5] By this act and this act alone does the celibate personality take on the "form" of the celibate life, just as the eye can be activated to its own proper act only by contact with light.

AFTERWORD
Celibacy and Priesthood

I am aware that celibacy is not required by the nature of the priesthood itself, that there is a long and venerable tradition of a married priesthood in the Byzantine and Orthodox Churches and that their expression of priesthood is no less valid that the Latin tradition.

No one pretends that the Western and Latin tradition is superior, only that it is different and I have tried to look at the vocation of celibacy from the viewpoint of a priest of the Latin Rite, with the clear understanding that the theology and spirituality of the Byzantine and Orthodox priest would be quite different. In these traditions, only bishops are required to be celibate and are usually chosen from monks who are celibate by their very profession. I have tried to make sense of the vocation to celibacy in the Western tradition.

The celibacy of the Latin Rite priest serves and supports a wide variety of pastoral and religious activities and so the celibate vocation has a wide variety of expressions. I have tried to get at the heart of the celibate commitment itself: that personal solitude where the priest cultivates an intense intimacy with God. Out of that personal solitude, the priest puts his hand to a vast spectrum of priestly and pastoral works and this personal solitude of celibacy is a critical factor in his effectiveness and in the creative freedom with which he works.

But what should be clear from this study of the celibate vocation is that intimacy with God in the solitude of celibacy must be a priority of his priestly existence and must be a primary occupation in which his total personality is rooted. Oddly enough, if the substance of his priestly existence is given to the intense cultivation of intimacy with God, the priest is inexhaustible, and the overflow into pastoral work is extensive, deep, and limitless. If the *substance* is given to the work itself, exhaustion and depression quickly set in and celibacy itself becomes a snare and an empty desert, with the priest's steps dogged by terrible loneliness and that harrowing emotional vacuum called "burn out", something resembling complete inertia.

Just as it would be tragic for the married man to neglect the intimacy of marriage in the name of dedication to job or profession and to court the very failure of the marriage itself in the name of this "work ethic", so the priest who neglects the cultivation of intimacy with God in the solitude of celibacy risks being saddled with mere professional competency or managerial effectiveness, with a growing distaste for pastoral work itself.

Every priest, from the first day he is ordained, senses something of the creative burning at the intense center of the celibate existence. He must grapple with the strange equations riveted into the very substance of his being. He must translate and interpret to himself the Divine impress that has seared itself into the very substance of his being. As he puts his hand to a multitude of priestly tasks, he comes to realize, if he has pondered his priesthood well, that what he *does* is not half so important as what he *is*, and that it is what he *is* that communicates something to people, not so much what he *does*.

But there is a *doing*, there is a task and it is more than the *complexus* of ritual and sacramental events that mark the life of a priest. The work of the priesthood is a uniquely *theological* task, it involves the cultivation of the larger identity of human beings, an identity which links them with an eternal and transcendent God. Men and women are more than inhabitants of the earth, they have a theological personality that reaches beyond the limits of their earthly personality, and it is this larger identity that is the proper province of the priest. Priestly and pastoral work is uniquely the *ars theologica*, the operational hand of a vibrant theological vision and an intense intimacy with God.

The creative possibilities of a vibrant and luminous priesthood are absolutely unlimited, but this pre-supposes that the priest is living at the deepest level of his being, that intense furnace of thought and insight where something resembling genius is born. There are no patterns for priestly effectiveness, there are no absolute models for pastoral theology. Every priest in a sense is in a land without any maps. He is in uncharted territory, and although the living example of the great priests who have gone before him can give inspiration and encouragement, the creative genius of his own work must be absolutely original.

The priest's involvement in the pastoral task is only by way of *overflow*. The very genius of pastoral work depends upon its flowing from a particular deep intimacy with God and, as in marriage, the intimacy is the very foundation of the lifestyle and is the exhilarating source of joy. Joy in God is at the very heart of priesthood, as joy in each other is at the very heart of marriage. Once the priest, indeed any celibate, has cultivated this intimacy with God, he can find God any time in any of His creatures; his joy in them becomes one and the same as the joy he finds in his more private moments of intimate communion. In marriage it is often true that as their love for each other matures, so does their appreciation for the source of all love, Love Himself; the more they understand what love is, the closer they are to God. The parallel between the two paths is astonishingly similar. Intimacy is the heart and center of any truly human life, and the priest remains a human being down to his fingertips.

The priest cannot simply be a professional among professionals and an administrator among administrators. He either becomes passionately involved with God, or he becomes passionately involved with prestige, or pride of position, or with trivial pursuits that merely amuse or entertain. Unless he is engaged with God on the deepest level of his being, the bulk of his personal investment will be placed elsewhere, with very little return on the investment.

In marriage the intimacy of the couple in their mutual solitude creates what can only be called a *paradisus conjugalis*, and it is from this intimate center and their continual experience of this intimacy, that is built the home, the family and the many activities and events of that home and family. And it is from his own personal solitude where he cultivates and experiences intimacy with God, what might be called the *paradisus sacerdotalis*, that the whole work of the priesthood proceeds. As in the intimacy of marriage, it is from his own intimacy with God that a fruitful and effective priesthood proceeds, the fruit of his own intimacy with God and the offspring of his own inner life.

The celibacy "problem", as this study has tried to show, has very little to do with the vocation to celibacy itself. That vocation is strong and well in thousands of priests and religious, and if there is a "crisis", the cause must be sought elsewhere. Much of the problem has to do with proper motivation: a healthy and wholesome attitude towards human sexuality and towards one's own sexuality, a sound anthropology at the heart of celibate spirituality, a positive grasp upon the essence of celibacy itself; a personal solitude which enables one to cultivate intimacy with God.

These are problems internal to celibacy itself, but if the nature of celibacy is as has been laid down in these pages it is also true that something must be done about the quality of the priestly life-style itself so that the celibate priest can have that privacy and that time that is needed for the cultivation of intimacy with God. The modern rectory is ill-equipped to provide this and if we want to see the cause of allures in the celibate vocation, that is the place to start. The modern rectory is simply not set up for privacy and for even that minimum of personal solitude that is needed for the cultivation of the celibate vocation. Some priests have been driven out of the priesthood simply by the sterility of the clerical culture and the sterility of the priest's own living conditions. A healthy marriage could not survive the turmoil and emptiness of the modern rectory and so it is no wonder that some priestly personalities collapse emotionally.

The question of motivation is also a critical question. The "Gothic" spirituality of the pre-Vatican II era placed absolutely no value upon human sexuality and the only judgments that were ever given in the sexual area were reduced to "concupiscence", "lust", or the conflict between "the flesh and the spirit." When one's own sexuality carries with it throughout a lifetime those kinds of labels, it is no wonder that some individuals crack under the strain of grappling with something they consider intrinsically evil. Without a wholesome acceptance of the inherent goodness of sexuality and of ones own sexuality in particular, celibacy becomes only a dark angel that stalks the inner recesses of the human psyche and strains human endurance to the breaking point.

Also, celibacy chosen under compulsion, whether moral, ascetic or spiritual, destroys the vocation to celibacy at its very roots and makes genuine growth in the celibate vocation highly unlikely. And this is not because of the strength of the "libido", or the effects of "concupiscence" upon the person of the priest. Sexual intimacy in marriage is a personal gift given to each individual human being by the very act of creation, and the renunciation of this gift must be so personal and so free that the stamp of one's own personal choice is placed upon the celibate vocation itself.

Sexual intimacy is not an exercise in "concupiscence" or an unspiritual indulgence in "the desires of the flesh." It is the crowning act of one's manhood, the finest, noblest and most genuine expression of one's masculinity or femininity, and the greatest earthly gift that God can give to a human being. Compulsion of any kind destroys the very nature of the celibate vocation, as it destroys the nature of marriage. Ecclesiastical authorities have not always been sensitive to the moral and spiritual compulsion embodied in certain "spiritualities". All that can be said of some older treatments of celibacy and some of the older seminary manuals is: "disgraceful." It could well be that in the present "celibacy crisis", the unsound spirituality of past days is catching up with us.

And there is another factor that those in charge of the education of the young should be well aware of: if you are asking a young man in the full bloom of manhood to give up the crowning act of his manhood and the noblest expression of his masculinity, you had better make that choice worthwhile by offering him more than just a clerical identity and a listing in the diocesan clergy directory. You had better provide him with the opportunity and freedom to give his best intelligence, his best efforts, his best energies and his best creative imagination to priestly work. Otherwise, there there would be no reason for him to exchange the love of a woman for anything so unpromising. Many of the young men of this generation have judged that the celibate priesthood "isn't worth it." And it is quite possible that under the present conditions under which many priests have to labor, they are right.

Perhaps harm has been done also by unfairly comparing celibacy and marriage. The subtle hint that celibacy is *better* because of the absence of genital sexual intimacy and that marriage is merely *good* because of the sex experience of the married man is unfair to both marriage and celibacy, because it fails to see the nature of both. The one ingredient common to both in this comparison is sexual intimacy, with the subtle hint that the choice of marriage is less generous because of this experience and celibacy is *superior* because it lacks it. However it may be stated, this is a subtle form of compulsion and it fails to see either the dignity of marriage and the inherent goodness of sexual intimacy, or the specific nature of the vocation to celibacy itself.

If the vocation to celibacy is ever to be born again in a new generation of religious, it must be born in total freedom, with no subtle put-downs of a love and an experience that mirrors in its sublimity God's own love for human beings. And I think it is time to cast aside the idea that vocations to celibacy are few because the young of this generation have a strong "libido" and are unwilling to make the "sacrifice" of sex in marriage to follow the celibate invitation of Christ. When the essence of celibacy is reduced to this, it is no wonder we have no takers.

Celibacy is founded, as I have tried to show in these pages, upon an intimacy as stunning and electrifying as the intimacy of marriage, and that takes nothing away from the beauty and wonder of married love. When we can discover and savor something of the ecstasy of priesthood and communicate to the young men of this generation that there is more to celibacy than "sleeping alone", then perhaps they will see that the loveliness of the bride-groom with the bride does not exhaust the human possibility and that there is a love-song as plaintive in its plea and as astonishing in its expectations as the love-song of bride and groom. It is that siren song that draws young men into the priesthood and unless they hear it loud and strong, they will listen to something else.

APPENDIX
The Theology of the Song of Songs

For centuries, there has been an intense debate among scholars about the "theology" of the *Song of Songs*, best exemplified in the controversy among Jewish Rabbis at the Council of Jamnia in 100. The debate at that time centered on whether the book should be included in the Hebrew Canon of the Scriptures and there were those who said it was unworthy because of its obvious sexual theme.

The defender of the book and its theme was the eminent Rabbi Akiva, who, along with Rashi and Maimonides, was considered one of the greatest of the Talmudic authorities, and, of the three, undoubtedly the most revered.

Akiva claimed that the love between a man and a woman and the sexual intimacy to which that love led, was eminently worthy of God and eminently worthy to be the subject of a book of the Scriptures:

> "God forbid that there should ever have been a dispute in Israel whether the Canticle is holy. The entire history of the world from its beginning to this very day does not outshine the day on which this book was given to Israel. All the Scriptures, indeed, are holy and sacred to the hands that touch them. But the Canticles are the Holy of Holies."

He meant that it was the sole Hebrew book in sacred use which concentrated wholly on the

109

theme of marital love between man and woman--this being the most important of all religious themes . . . prompting a recognition of a deeper love between God and man.[1]

There have been many excellent mystical interpretaions of the *Song* through the centuries, and, indeed, it serves also to describe the experience of an individual's intimacy with God. But for our purposes here, the imagery and vivid language of this book provide a true education in sexuality and communicate with all the authority of Divine Revelation a view of the sexual intimacy of man and woman in marriage. In life and in literature, and in the conversation of people, the image of sex and sexuality is not always a noble one, and the intimate association of man and woman in marriage, in all its sexual wonder, has often been reduced to something low and degrading.

The *Song* communicates the eminent dignity of sexual intimacy and the sheer beauty of sexual love in all its intimate expressions. It is shown to be an activity and an experience eminently worthy and desirable, the crowning act of manhood and of womanhood, the finest and most genuine expression of masculinity and femininity, and the unique expression of love between a man and a woman.

Part of the problem is that, historically, theologians and spiritual writers have had a very low opinion of sexuality itself and its intimate expression in marriage. And even writers untainted with any hint of Puritanism, look upon this exaltation of marital love as exaggerated.

Dietrich von Hildebrand, in the book so often quoted in this study, completely disagrees with this typically "celibate" point of view:

> . . . The love between a man and a woman is not a romantic invention of poets, but a tremendous factor in human life from the very beginning of the history of mankind, the source of the deepest happiness in human earthly life . . . Indeed it is this love alone which is the key for an understanding of the true nature of sex, of its value and of the mystery which it embodies.[2]

In one sense, the purpose of the "theology" of the *Song of Songs* for us is to change our low view of sexual love and see it as truly the greatest earthly gift that God has given to the human race and to put human beings completely at ease with their sexuality and with its most intimate expression.

Nor is this view of sexuality, and of the intimacy to which it leads, in any way a danger to celibacy, since the gift of sexuality, as this study has tried to show, is an integral part of the human personality and the human inheritance of the celibate. He freely deprives himself of this crowning act of his masculinity, or she her femininity, but neither should have doubt about the inherent goodness of the gift and the activity forsaken, and, what can truly be called the shattering significance of this gift in the experience of men and women.

What is proclaimed in the book in language alive with poetry and beauty is the inherent goodness of human sexuality and of its joyful and intimate expression in marriage. And so the imagery has a twofold purpose: to communicate the sheer loveliness of the love between a man and a woman and to use that vivid imagery to indicate the tenderness and wonder of God's love and something of the expectation His own lovers can have in their intimacy with Him.

The *Song of Songs* is an important theological source for it is the only book of the Scriptures that treats so specifically of love between man and woman. It is the richest source for a theology of human sexuality and for the experience of sex in marriage and is so intense in its exaltation of sexual love that many early Jewish and Christian commentators saw only an allegorical meaning in its vivid imagery. Modern scholars, however, take it in its literal meaning[3], a superb hymn to the sexual love of man and woman and the joyful expectations that the hand of God Himself has imbedded in the love of man and woman.

In Jewish history, the *Song of Songs* was a handbook of marital love and revealed to young lovers the depth and intensity of their own expectations in marriage. It was Akiva's deep and tender love for his wife, Rachel, whom he had married when they both were very young[4], that moved him to defend the theme of the canticle. His only objection to its secular use was reading it and proclaiming it in taverns, which he thought unfitting. Apparently, he expected young married couples to have it in their hands on their wedding night.

NOTES

KEY TO ABBREVIATIONS FOR REFERENCES TO THE WORKS OF THOMAS AQUINAS:

S.T. = Summa Theologica

De Boetii de Trin. = Commentary on Boethius' on the Trinity.

S.C.G. = Summa Contra Gentiles

Q.D. de Virt = Questiones Disputatae de veritate

ad Corinth = Commentary on the Second Letter to the Corinthians

Principium = Thomas' Innaugural Address given in 1256 to his confreres in Paris upon becoming a Master at the University of Paris. See P. Mandonnet's dition of Thomas's Opuscula Omnia IV (Paris, 1927), pp. 491-6 for further reference.

The references: I-II, II-II, etc. refer to places in the Summa.

NOTES TO ESSAY I

1   von Hildebrand, op. Cit.
2   Ibid.
3   Ibid.
4   See von Hildebrand's Man and Woman, Franciscan Herald Press, Chicago, 1966.
5   von Hildebrand, op. cit.
6   See Appendix.
7   Gaudium et Spes, para. 49.
8   Ibid.
9   For a description and analysis of the Gnostic pessimism referred to here, see F.E. Peters' Harvest of Helenism, Simon & Schuster, New   York, 1970.
10 See Thomas' Summa Theologica, Question 98.

NOTES TO ESSAY II

1 Von Hidebrand, op. cit.
2 Ibid.
3 Ibid.
4 Gaudium et Spes, para. 49.

NOTES TO ESSAY III

1 In Boet. De Trin: "A man already possesses some shre in the rue beatitude according to the measure in which he studies wisdom." --S.C.G., I, 2. "By wisdom itself is one led to the everlasting kingdom."--S.C.G., I., 2.
2 S.T. II-II, Q. 180.

NOTES TO ESSAY V

1 Gerard Manley Hopkins, "The Wreck of the Deutschland", from The Poems of Gerard Manley Hopkins, Oxford University Press, New York, 1984.
3 Expos. De Divin. Nom., I, lect. 3.
4 S.C.G., I.
5 Expos. De Divin. Nom., I, lect. 3.
6 S.T., II-II, Q. 182.

NOTES TO ESSAY VI

1 Brother Antoninus, "A Canticle to the Christ in the Holy Eucharist". This poem can be found in Today's Poets: American and British Poetry Since the 1930's, ed. Chad Walsh, Charles Scribner's Sons, New York, 1964.
2 Notes for an Autobiography, op. cit.
3 Brother Antoninus, op. cit.

NOTES TO ESSAY VII

1 Josef Pieper, LEISURE The Basis of Culture, Pantheon Books, New York, 1952, pg.29.

2 Cf. the author's article "Father Flanagan of Boys Town" published in America magazine, Nov. 8, 1986. Also in a sketch of the same title in Portraits of Faith, Our Sunday Visitor Press, Huntington, Indiana, 1974.

NOTES TO ESSAY VIII

1 Hopkins, op. cit.

2 The World Tresury of Children's Literature, 3 vols. ed. Clifton Fadiman, Little, Brown, & Co., Boston, 1984

3 Ibid., vol 3, pg. 604.

4 Ibid. vol. 1, pg. xiv.

5 Ibid.

6 Harvey Egan, op. cit. See also his Christian Mysticism: the Future of a Tradition, Pueblo Publishing Co., 1984.

NOTES TO ESSAY IX

1 De Boetii de Trin., Prem. Q. 2, resp.

2 Cf. "Belief Today", by Bernard Lonergan, S.J. in Schema XIII Magazine, vol. 1. no. 1, Jan-Feb, 1970.

3 See Pieper, op. cit.

4 Ibid.

5 Ibid.

NOTES TO APPENDIX

1   Robert Graves, The Song of Songs, Text and Commentary, Crown Publishers Inc., New York, 1973, pg 3.

2   von Hildebrand, op. cit.

3   See Marvin Pope's proem. to the Song of Songs in the Anchor Bible, Doublday, Garden City, New York, 1964.

4   Cf. Louis Finkelstein, Akiba: Scholar, Saint and Martyr, Atheneum, New York, 1985, pgs. 22ff, 79ff.

Additional books in the
SCHUYLER SPIRITUAL SERIES